GEOGRAPHY AND HISTORY SECONDARY

BY ME

Cristina Granda Gallego
Raúl Núñez Heras
Clara Mimbrera Olarte

PHYSICAL GEOGRAPHY

Contents

00 Getting started 4

01 Planet Earth 6

1. The Earth 8
2. The movements of the Earth 10
3. Orientation and location 14
4. The representation of the Earth 16

Discovery techniques: Interpreting a map 18

Read and think: How does a GPS receiver work? 22

02 Geosphere: Relief and landforms 24

1. The internal structure of the Earth 26
2. Relief formation 28
3. Types of relief 30
4. The Earth's continents 34

Discovery techniques: Geographical graphs and charts 36

Read and think: Sand or pebbles? 40

03 The Earth's surface 42

1. Land relief in Spain 44
2. Land relief in Europe 48
3. Land relief in Africa 50
4. Land relief in America 52
5. Land relief in Asia 54
6. Land relief in Oceania and Antarctica 55

Discovery techniques: How to interpret a topographic map 56

Read and think: The gold rush 60

04 The hydrosphere 62

1. The hydrosphere 64
2. The distribution of water on Earth 65
3. The distribution of water in Spain 68
4. The distribution of water in Europe 72
5. The distribution of water in the rest of the world 74

Discovery techniques: River profiles 76

Read and think: Why are clouds sometimes white and sometimes grey? 80

05 Atmosphere: Weather and climate 82

1. The Earth's atmosphere 84
2. The properties of air 85
3. Atmospheric dynamics 86
4. The Earth's climates 88
5. Climates in Europe 92
6. Climates in Spain 94

Discovery techniques: Making and interpreting a climograph 96

Read and think: The *gota fría* 100

06 The Earth's biomes 102

1. The Earth's biomes 104
2. Biomes in Europe 110
3. Biomes in Spain 112
4. Humans and the environment 114

Discovery techniques: Creating and reading topic maps 118

Read and think: Climate change and life on Earth 122

Glossary 124

Big thinkers 128

ARABIA

What is geography?

0.1 The concept of geography

Geography is the science that deals with the study of the Earth. It describes and analyses the phenomena that take place on the Earth's surface, and the Earth's relationship with the spaces around it. The aim is to analyse and find out about the natural environment and the changes and transformations that occur through human activity.

Geographers study these things from two perspectives:

- **Regional geography**. The study of a particular geographical space, whether it's a country or a continent.
- **General geography**. The Earth is seen as a unit, with subcategories that we can study separately.

SUBDIVISIONS OF GENERAL GEOGRAPHY

Physical geography

This is the study of the Earth's physical environment in its different forms: the relief, its bodies of water, the atmosphere, etc.

Human geography

This is the analysis of human activities (such as economics or population trends) in relation to the natural environment.

0.2 The analysis of space

Geographers use a variety of **sources and tools** to describe and interpret geographical space.

GEOGRAPHICAL SOURCES

Using **direct sources** involves observing the physical space which you want to analyse. This method is known as fieldwork, and involves field measurements, collecting plant and mineral samples, etc.

In order to carry out their studies, geographers make use of other sciences, such as physics, biology and economics.

Indirect or secondary sources are produced through the collection and analysis of information. They include maps, statistical data, written sources (reports, books, descriptions) and visual sources, such as photographs.

0.3 Geographical space

The geographer's object of study is geographical space and everything which has an impact on it. The concept of space can be understood in various ways.

CHARACTERISTICS OF GEOGRAPHICAL SPACES

Given that geographical space is not something static, geographers also study the changes that take place in it.

CHANGES IN GEOGRAPHICAL SPACE

Changes caused by **natural phenomena**.

These changes can take place within a short period of time, such as those caused by a volcanic eruption, or over a much longer period, such as the erosion caused by the wind or the rain.

Changes caused by **human activity**.

These changes are called 'anthropic actions' and are usually clearly visible in terms of their impact on the landscape. Common examples of such changes include the effects of crop cultivation and infrastructural development.

NATURAL LANDSCAPES AND MODIFIED LANDSCAPES

Unspoilt natural landscapes are a rarity on Earth. Most of the Earth's surface has been changed through human activity. Secondary sources, such as photographs, are very useful for analysing these changes.

01 Planet Earth

LOOKING BACK

- What are the names of the planets in the Solar System?
- What galaxy is the Solar System in?
- How long does it take the Earth to rotate on its axis?
- How long does it take the Earth to orbit the Sun?
- What is geography?
- What do we use maps for?

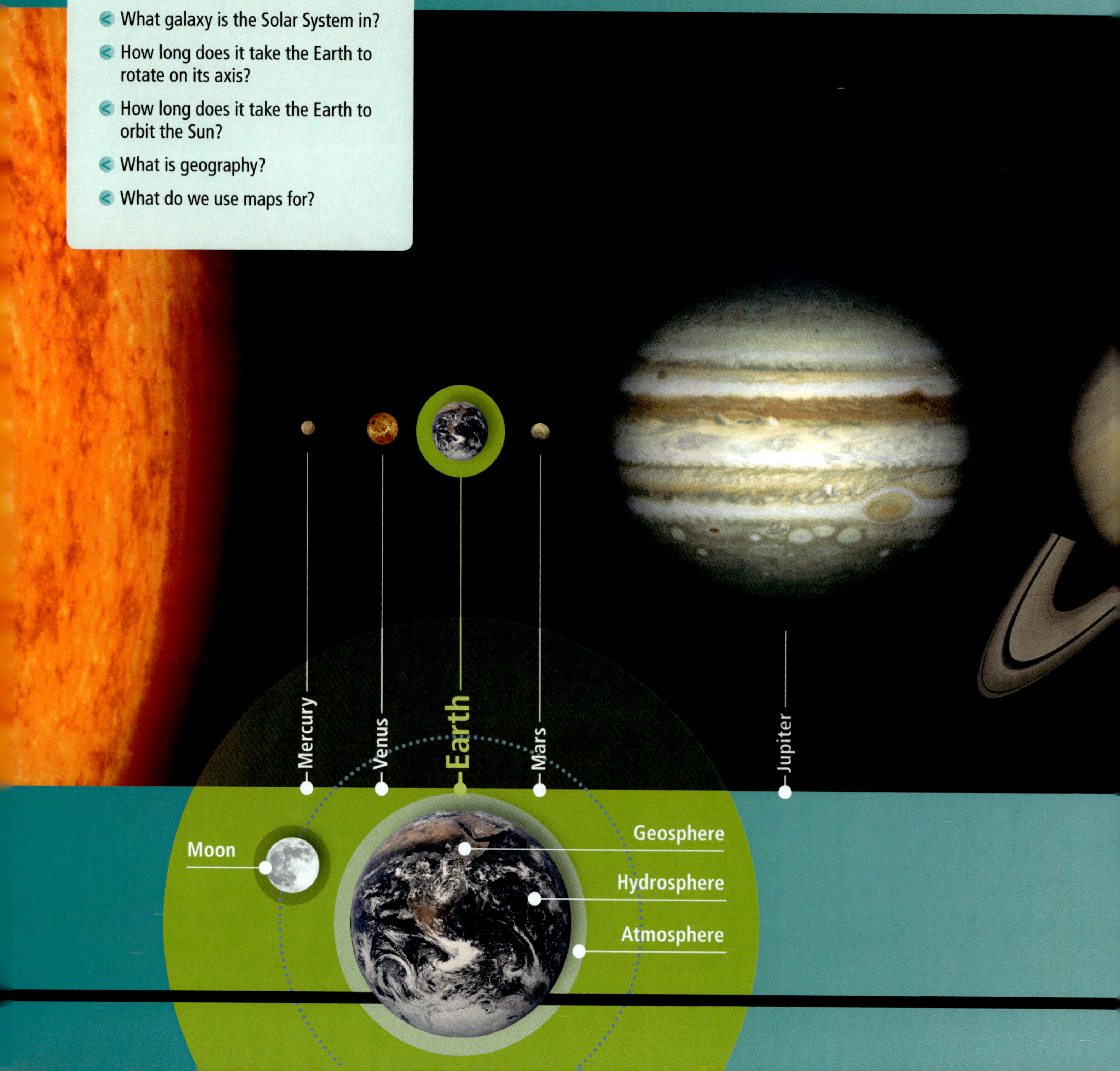

The universe in fiction

It was as early as the 2nd century A.D. that Lucian of Samasota, a Greek-speaking Syrian, wrote the first known work considered as science fiction. In True History, a whirlwind lifts up Lucian's ship and takes him and his companions to the Moon.

They become involved in a **fierce** war between the King of the Moon and the King of the Sun, who both want to colonise the Morning Star (Venus). In the end, the Sun wins the war by covering the Moon with clouds.

In the novel, the Sun, the Moon, the planets and the stars have different geographical **features** and their inhabitants are different too. Strange creatures, such as men with dogs' faces and centaurs made of clouds, form the armies.

- What is the difference between planets and stars?
- What do we know about the **inhabitants** of other planets today?

LOOKING FORWARD

- What is the Universe made up of?
- What causes the seasons?
- How do we locate places on the Earth?
- How do cartographers collect the data they need to make maps?
- What information does a map include to help us interpret it?

1 The Earth

What is the Universe made up of?

1.1 The Earth in the Solar System

The Earth is a planet that is part of the Solar System. This system is formed by a group of planets, dwarf planets, satellites, and other celestial bodies that **revolve** around a star: the Sun.

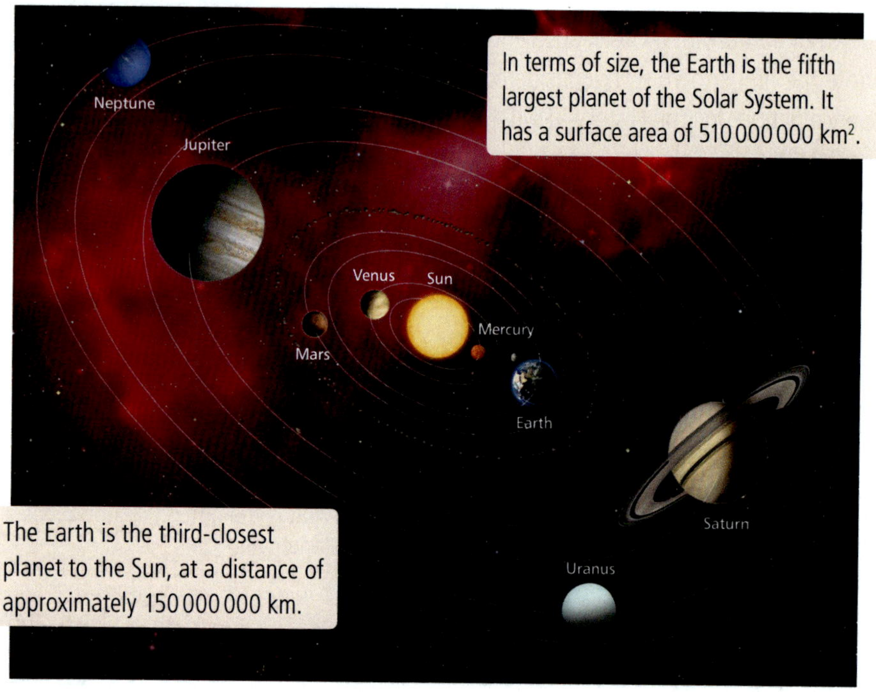

In terms of size, the Earth is the fifth largest planet of the Solar System. It has a surface area of 510 000 000 km^2.

The Earth is the third-closest planet to the Sun, at a distance of approximately 150 000 000 km.

BIG THINKER

Heidi Hammel is a planetary **astronomer** who specialises in the giant planets Neptune and Uranus. She was a member of the team that first saw Neptune's Great Dark Spot, a huge storm as big as Earth. Her research on other planets is helping us understand our planet much better.

1.2 The Earth: a habitable planet

The Earth is unique because it is the only planet that we know can support life. The existence of a great variety of life on Earth is down to the following:

- Temperatures which are neither extremely cold nor extremely hot. On other planets, temperatures can reach hundreds of degrees Celsius above or below zero.
- A gaseous layer, called the atmosphere, which provides oxygen and protects us from solar radiation.
- Large amounts of water: three-quarters of the planet is covered by water.

THE EARTH

The Earth is a sphere, but not a perfect one as it is flattened at the poles. This shape is called a **geoid**.

The widest part of the planet is the equator: an imaginary line that divides the Earth in two halves called *hemispheres*.

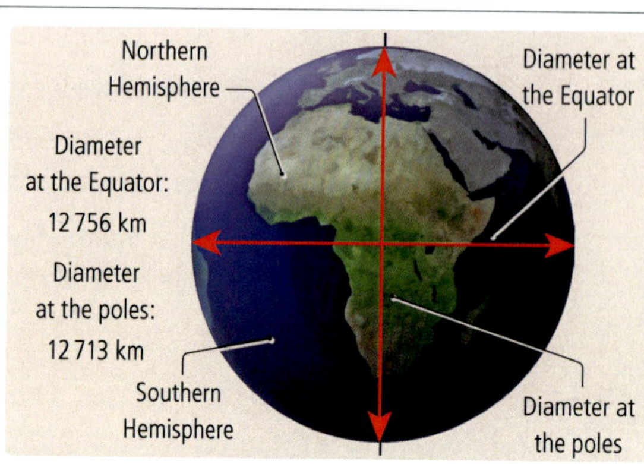

ACTIVITIES

1. Indicate which three physical conditions determine the existence of life on Earth. Then explain how each one of them influences the existence of living creatures.
2. Investigate: What is a satellite? What is Earth's satellite called? Which planet has the highest number of satellites? Name some of them.
3. The Earth is in the shape of a geoid. What does this mean?

1.3 The elements of the Earth

Our planet is formed of solid, liquid and gas elements. They are grouped into three categories: the atmosphere, the hydrosphere and the geosphere.

ATMOSPHERE

The atmosphere is the layer that surrounds the Earth. It is formed of a group of gases, water vapour and tiny particles in the air. It is essential for life and the main meteorological processes happen there.

The atmosphere is organised into several layers.

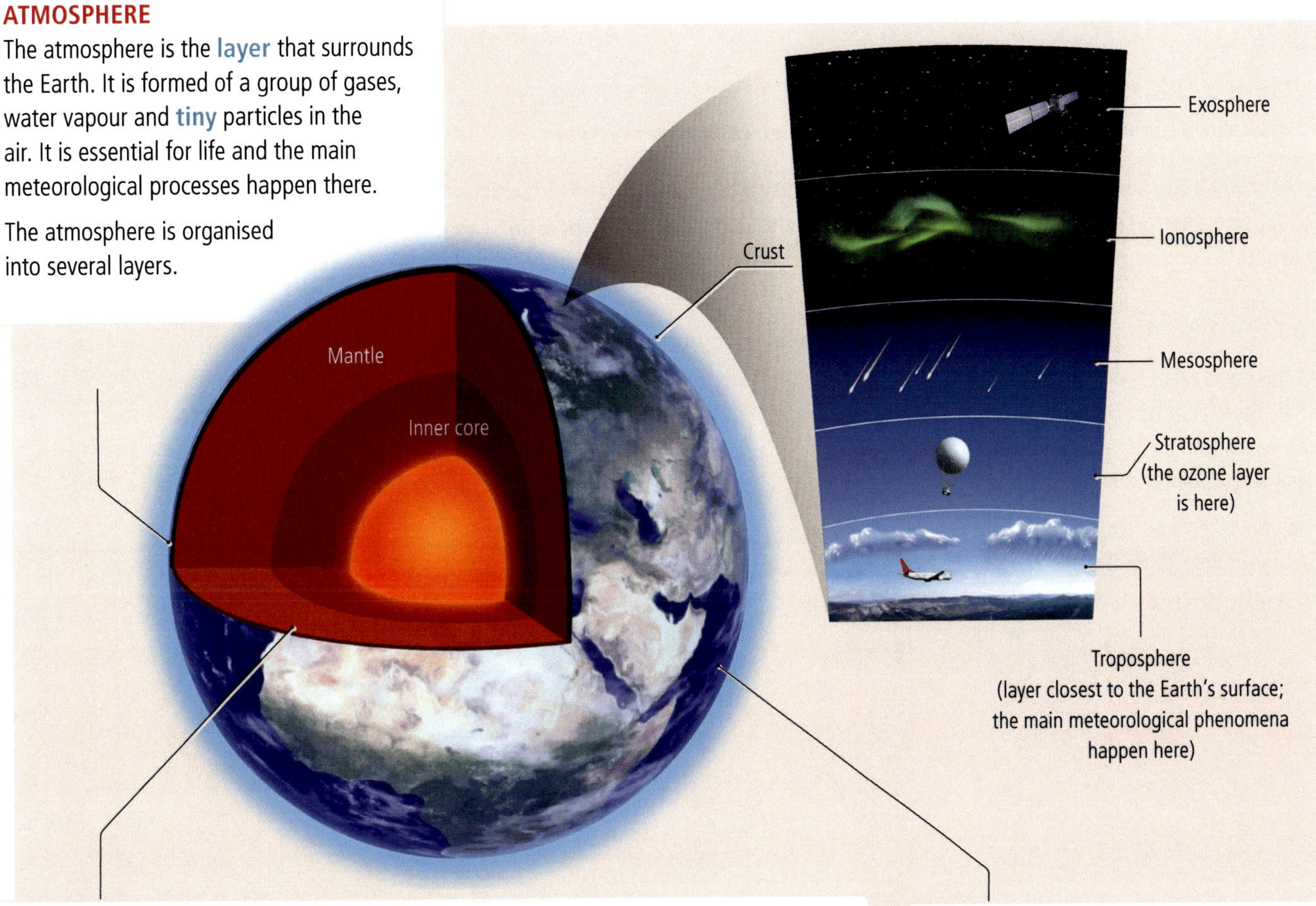

GEOSPHERE

The geosphere is formed by solid elements. It includes most of the planet and is divided into three layers:

- The **crust** is the largest and thinnest layer of the Earth. It is made out of solid rock. In this layer we can find sea floors and the continents that emerge from the oceans.
- The **mantle** is the middle layer. We can find melted rock in it called magma. We can also distinguish two parts: the upper mantle and the lower mantle.
- The **inner core** is the deepest layer. We know comparatively little about it. It is thought to be made of very heavy minerals that appear in a viscous state in its outer and a solid state in its inner section.

HYDROSPHERE

The hydrosphere is the total amount of water existent on Earth. Most of the water is salty, like that from oceans and seas. The rest is fresh water and most of this is found in the ice caps. We also find fresh water in rivers, lakes, glaciers and in groundwater.

ACTIVITIES

4. Define *hydrosphere* and explain why the Earth is called 'the blue planet'.
5. Define *atmosphere* and write down the elements that form it.
6. Observe the illustration and answer the questions:
   a. What three layers make up the geosphere?
   b. Explain what can be found in the Earth's crust.
   c. What is magma? In which layer of the geosphere can it be found?
   d. What materials is the inner core formed of?

2 The movements of the Earth

The Earth moves through space in two different ways: rotation and revolution.

2.1 Rotation

The Earth rotates on its own axis. It takes the Earth 24 hours to complete one full rotation. This movement produces the sequence of nights and days.

As the Earth rotates on its axis, one side is lit by the Sun: on this side it is day. At the same time the other side is not lit by the Sun: on this side it is night.

TIME ZONES

As the Earth takes 24 hours to rotate 360°, the planet has been divided into 24 time zones. Consequently, 15° represents a difference of one hour.

The imaginary lines dividing the Earth into time zones are not always straight. There can be territorial, political or commercial reasons for this.

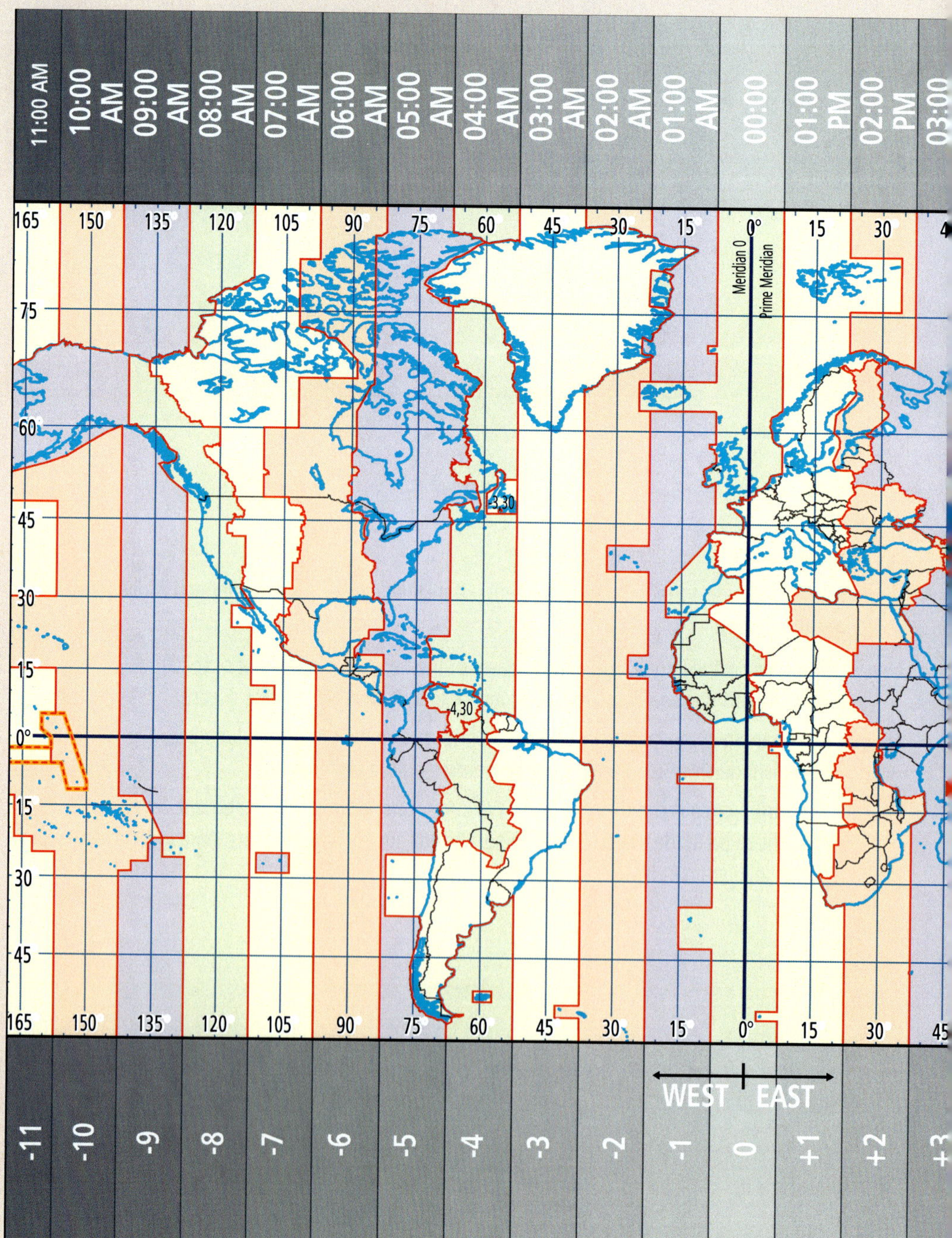

What causes the seasons?

The Earth rotates once in about 24 hours with respect to the Sun and once every 23 hours, 56 minutes and 4 seconds with respect to the stars. Earth's rotation is slowing slightly with time; thus, a day was shorter in the past. This is due to the tidal effects the Moon has on Earth's rotation.

To calculate the time difference starting from the Prime Meridian:

- We add an hour every 15° if we are moving to the east.
- We subtract an hour every 15° if we are moving to the west.

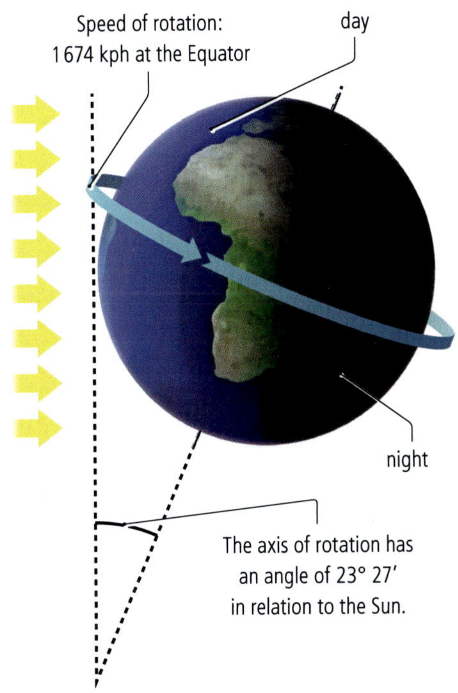

ACTIVITIES

7. Look at the map of time zones. If it is 12 noon in the United Kingdom, what time is it in 1) Managua, 2) Moscow and 3) Bangkok?

8. Think. At the end of the 19th century, the use of trains made time zones necessary. Can you explain why?

2.2 Revolution

The revolution of the Earth is its elliptical orbit around the Sun. It takes the Earth one year to orbit the Sun. One year is exactly 365 days, 5 hours, 48 minutes and 45 seconds.

This movement has an important consequence: the changing of the seasons. Seasons are the four periods into which the year is divided. They begin as the Sun passes through a solstice or an equinox. Each season has different climatic conditions that result from the different intensity of sunlight the Earth's surface receives during the revolution movement.

THE REVOLUTION OF THE EARTH AND THE SEASONS

The seasons are the result of:

- The tilt of the Earth's axis.
- The revolution of the Earth around the Sun.

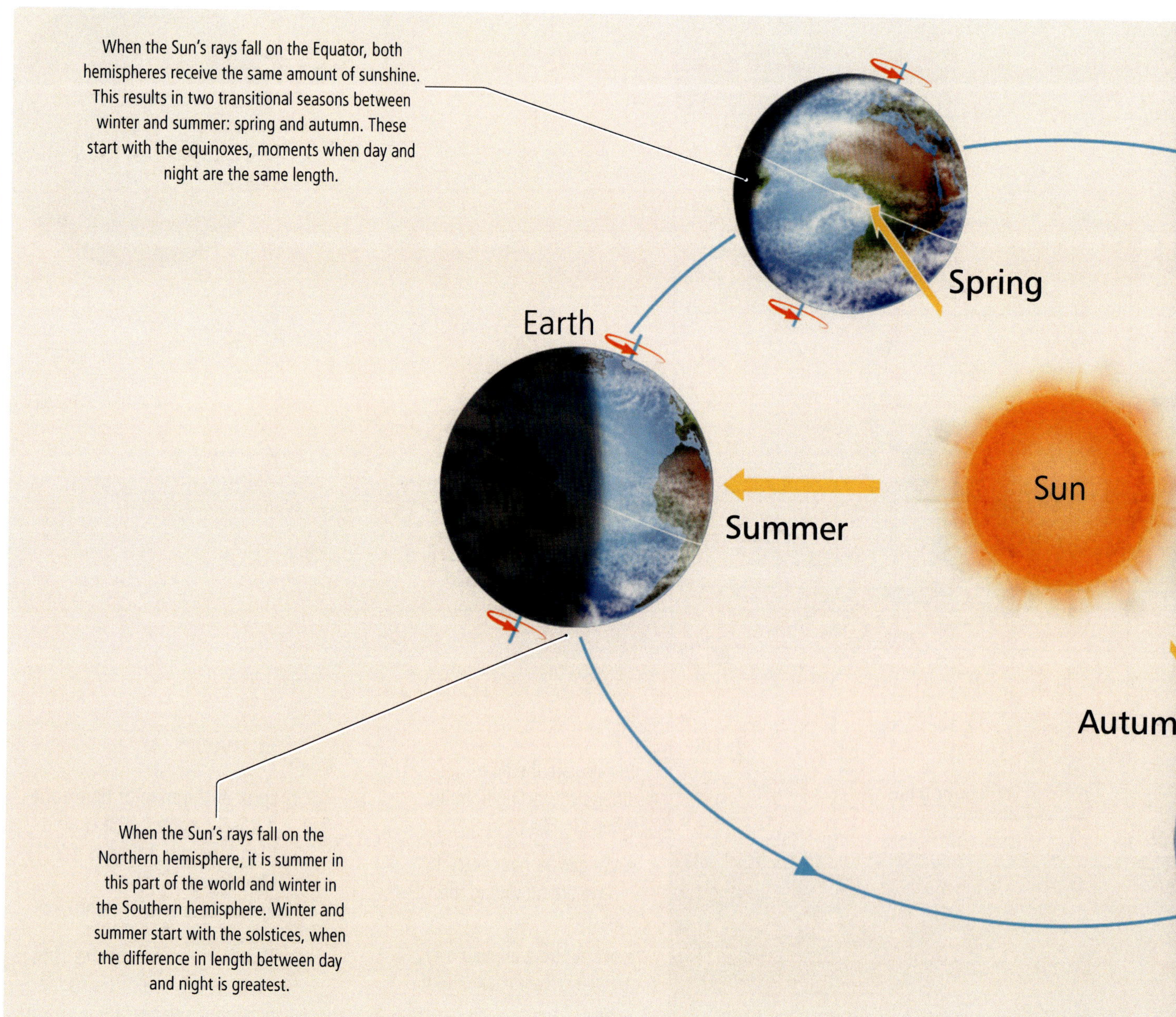

Also, the inclination of the Earth's axis prevents the solar rays from reaching the Northern and Southern hemispheres in the same way. This is why seasons occur at opposing times of the year in each hemisphere.

Many parts of the Earth experience changing seasons. The warm spring brings new flowers. This is followed by a hot summer filled with holidays and outdoor swimming. Following it there is another warm season known as autumn, where leaves turn beautiful shades of reds and browns before falling from their trees. Finally, after all of these warmer seasons, comes the winter, the coldest season.

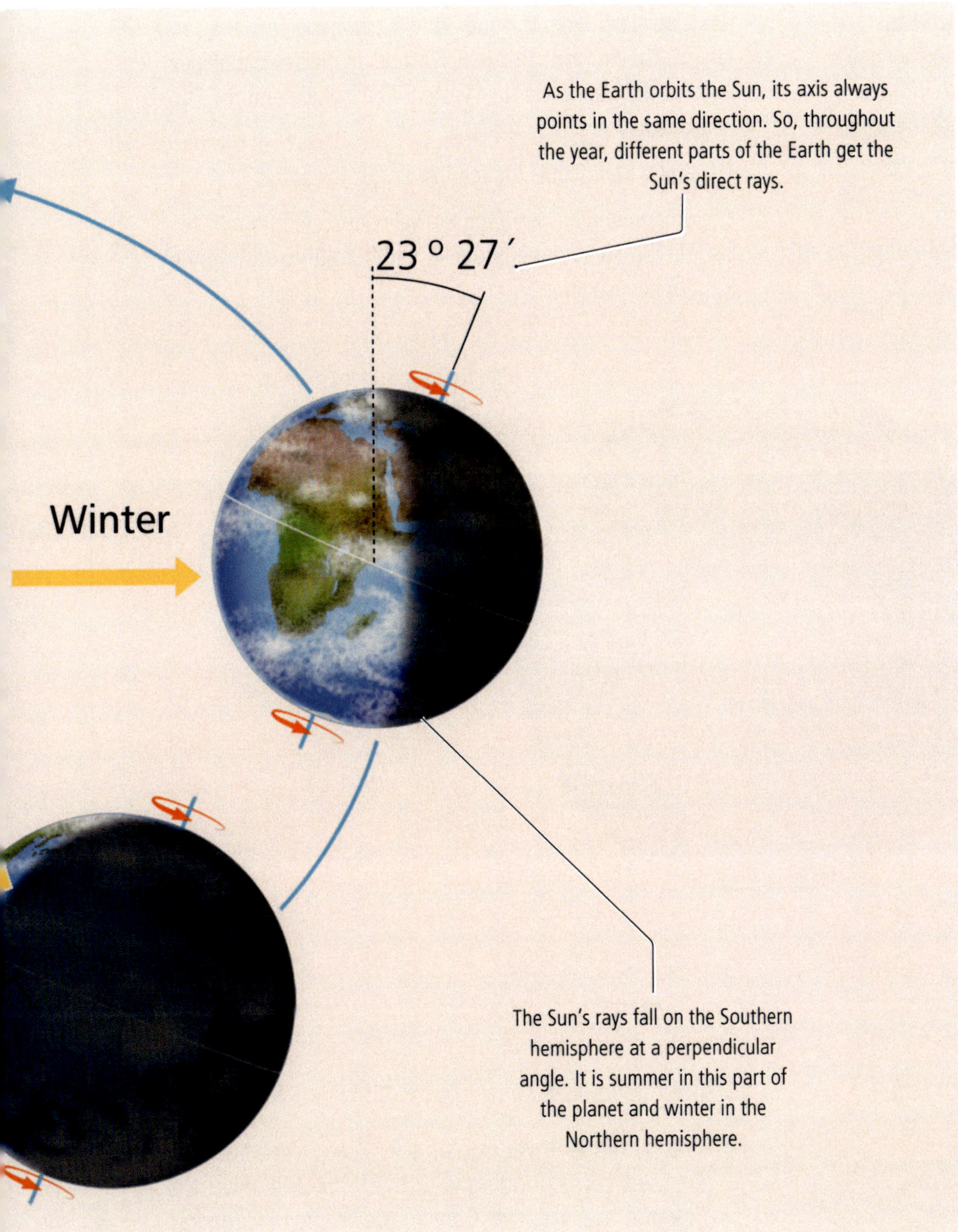

THE FOUR SEASONS

Spring

Summer

Autumn

Winter

ACTIVITIES

9. Explain what the Earth's revolution movement consists of and indicate its duration. What consequences does this movement have?
10. In what countries does it get darker before Spain – in those that are to the east of our country or those that are to the west? Explain your answer by indicating which elements influence this fact.

3 Orientation and location

➲ How do we locate places on the Earth?

ORIENTATION

We can locate places on the Earth using the four cardinal points: north, south, east and west. This is a result of the Earth's rotation and the sequence of nights and days. The Earth rotates towards the east, and so the Sun rises in the east and sets in the west. North and south signal the direction of the Earth's axis.

LOCATION

The cardinal points determine directions. However, to locate a specific point on the Earth's surface, we use a **grid** of imaginary lines. These imaginary lines are called parallels and meridians.

Parallels (or lines of latitude) are imaginary lines that run from east to west and are perpendicular to the meridians and parallel to the Equator. The Equator is an imaginary line **equidistant** from the poles that divides the Earth into two hemispheres: the Northern hemisphere and the Southern hemisphere.

The Equator is the parallel at 0° latitude.

The rest of the parallels are progressively numbered from 0° to 90° in both the Northern and Southern hemispheres.

Meridians (or lines of longitude) are imaginary lines that run from North Pole to South Pole. Each meridian is the same length. The Prime or Greenwich Meridian divides the planet into two hemispheres: the Western hemisphere and the Eastern hemisphere.

The Prime Meridian is the meridian at 0° longitude.

The other meridians are progressively numbered from 0° to 180° in the Western hemisphere, and from 0° to 180° in the Eastern hemisphere.

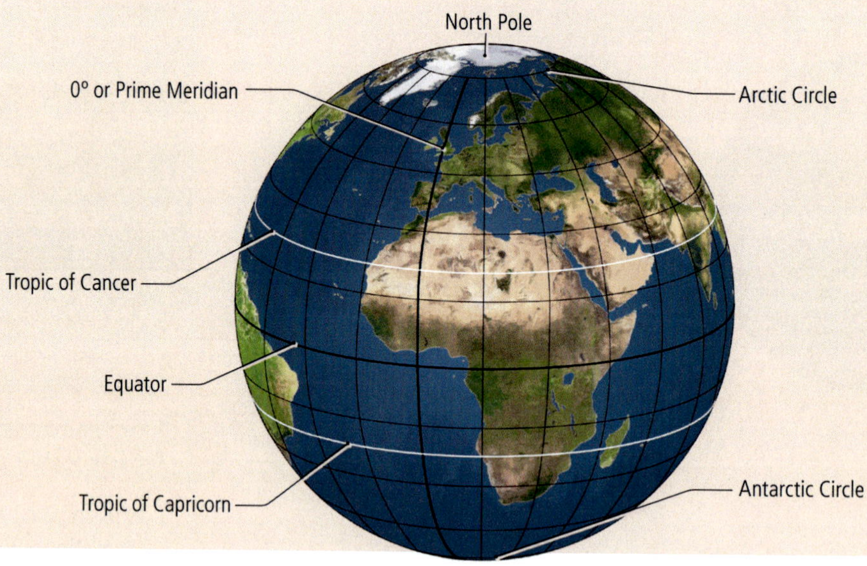

ACTIVITIES

11. What is the difference between a solstice and an equinox? How are both related to seasons?

12. Compare and contrast parallels and meridians. Then, do the same with longitude and latitude.

13. Are the parallels the same length? If so, why?

14. Draw a globe in your notebook. Then, trace and label the lines corresponding with the Prime Meridian, the Equator, the Tropic of Cancer, the Tropic of Capricorn, the Arctic Circle and the Antarctic Circle.

GEOGRAPHIC COORDINATES

Geographic coordinates are used to define the position of a specific point on the Earth using degrees. To find out the geographic coordinates of a specific point we need to combine latitude and longitude:

Latitude is the angular distance between any point on the Earth's surface and the Equator. It is measured in degrees.

Latitude runs from 0° at the Equator to 90° at the North and South poles.

Longitude is the angular distance between any point on the Earth's surface and the Prime Meridian.

Longitude is 0° if the point is located on the Prime Meridian, that passes through Greenwich, England. Longitude is measured as an angle east or west from the Prime Meridian. Longitude starts from 0° at the Prime Meridian to +180° to the east and –180° to the west.

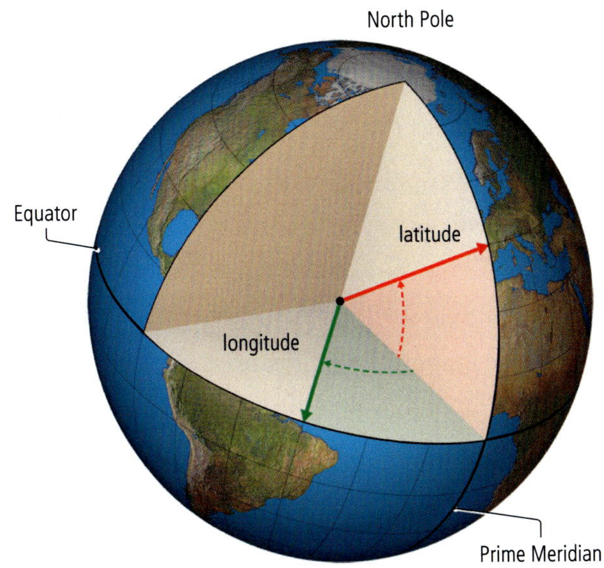

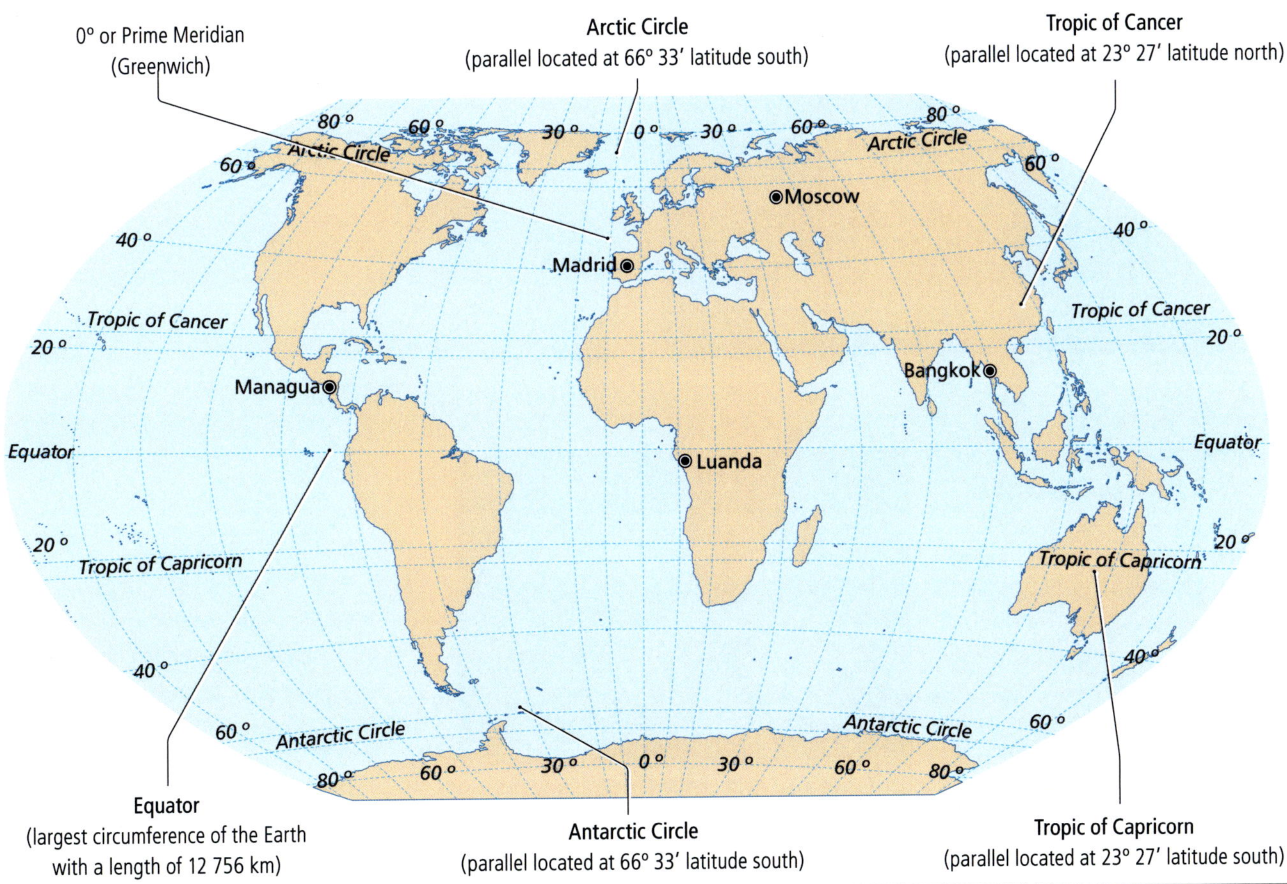

ACTIVITIES

15. Define the concept of latitude. Where is latitude 0°? What is the maximum latitude that can be located? Show where we can find the maximum latitudes on the planet.

16. Define the concept of longitude. Where can we find longitude 0°? What is the maximum longitude that can be located? Show where we can find the maximum longitudes on the planet.

4 The representation of the Earth

How do cartographers collect the data they need to make maps?

We use **maps** to represent geographical space. A map is a representation of the Earth or a part of it on a flat surface or plane.

Cartography is the study and making of maps. **Cartographic resources** and projection are used.

4.1 Cartographic resources

Today, the most common techniques used to study the Earth are:

PHOTO INTERPRETATION

This uses photographs of the Earth taken from aeroplanes at different heights and angles. These photographs make it possible to modify old maps and draw new ones.

Photograph taken from an aeroplane

REMOTE SENSING

This system obtains information about the Earth's surface using cameras on aeroplanes and satellites that sense and record reflected or emitted energy. This technique can be used to obtain temperatures, for example.

Processing and analysing this information gives us precise knowledge of the Earth's surface.

Satellite image of the Iberian Peninsula

A GEOGRAPHIC INFORMATION SYSTEM (GIS)

This is a computer system designed to capture, store, manipulate, analyse, manage and present all types of geographical data. A GIS allows us to relate different information in a spatial context and to reach conclusions.

Global positioning system (GPS) device

SATELLITES AND THE WEATHER

Some satellites carry instruments that can measure the surface temperature of oceans and seas – like thermometers in the sky.

This information is important for weather forecasting and research on climate change.

ACTIVITIES

17. List the inventions and technology which have made it easier to make maps. Note down the purpose of each item.

18. How do you think maps were made before aerial photography existed? Discuss the advantages of this new type of photography.

19. Which of the three techniques would you use to…

a. learn about climates?

b. study the course of a river?

c. present different kinds of data on one map?

4.2 Cartographic projections

The Earth has an irregular shape, called a geoid. A globe is the most accurate representation of the Earth's surface. That is why representing the Earth on a flat map creates a number of difficulties. We need to use projection systems to represent the Earth on maps as accurately as possible.

There are different types of projections:

CONIC PROJECTION

The surface of the Earth is projected on an imaginary cone. Its axis coincides with the axis of the Earth's rotation.

This system is mainly used to represent temperate and polar regions because the further we move down the map, the more distorted and less accurate it becomes.

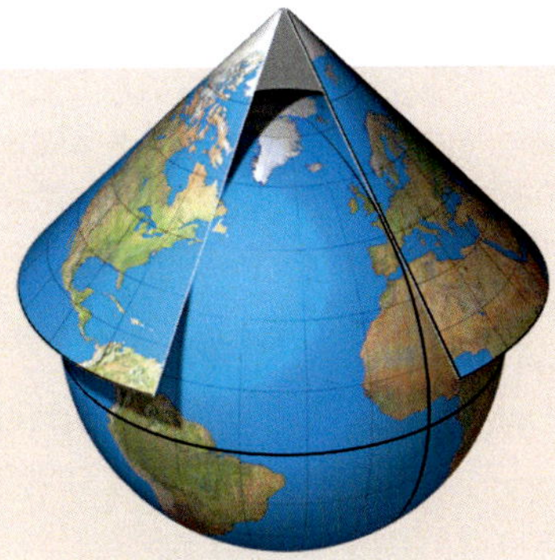

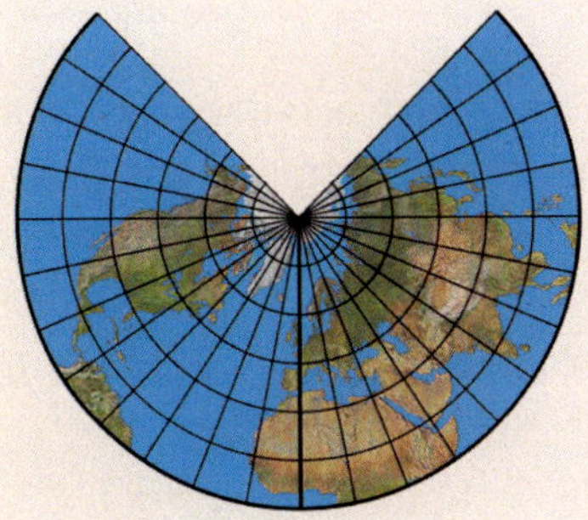

PLANE PROJECTION

The image is obtained from a flat surface placed on one of the polar regions. In this type of projection, we obtain a circular representation with one of the poles in the centre. Consequently, it is mainly used to represent the polar regions.

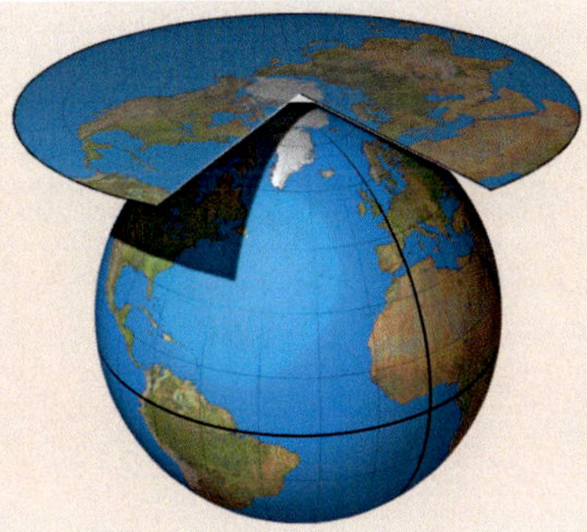

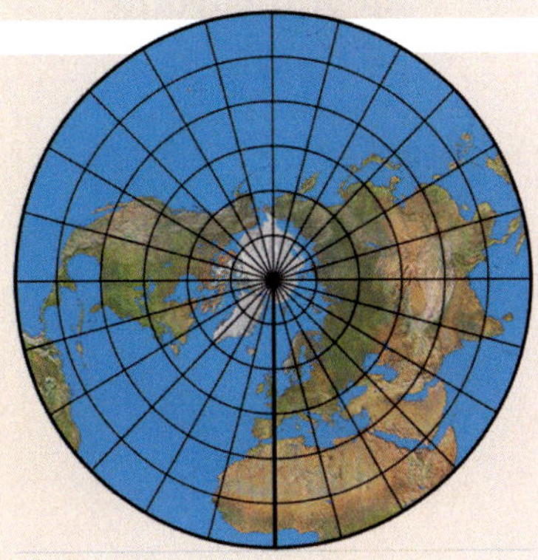

CYLINDRICAL PROJECTION

The surface of the Earth is projected on an imaginary cylinder around the Earth. A cylindrical projection map is the most common type of map we see of the whole planet. However, the closer to the poles we move, the more distorted the proportions of the map become.

The best-known cylindrical map was made by Mercator in the 16th century. However, the areas furthest away from the Equator are distorted in this projection.

In order to try to solve this problem, in 1974 James Gall and Arno Peters developed a projection that respects the real size of the continents.

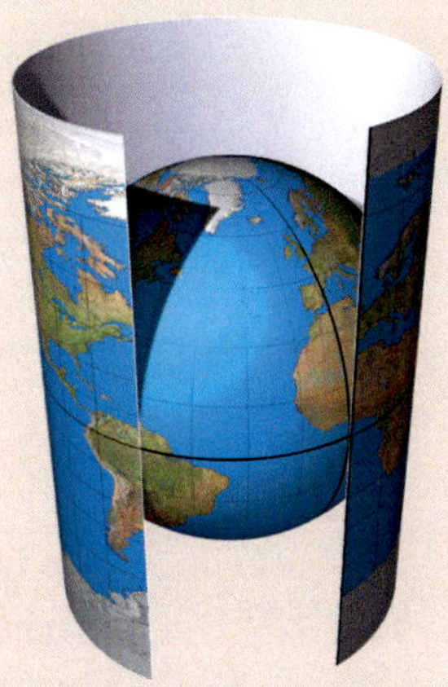

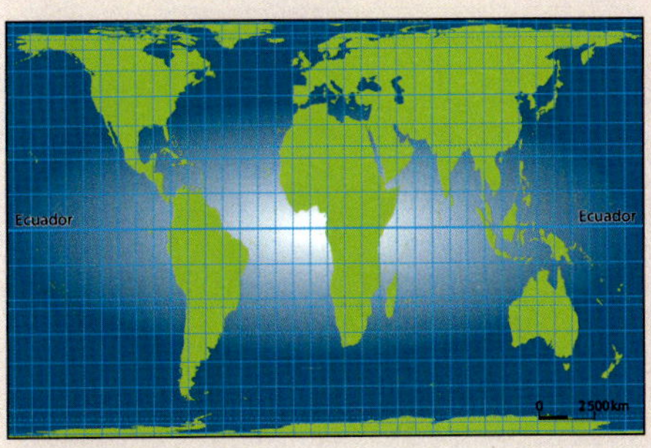

Peters projection

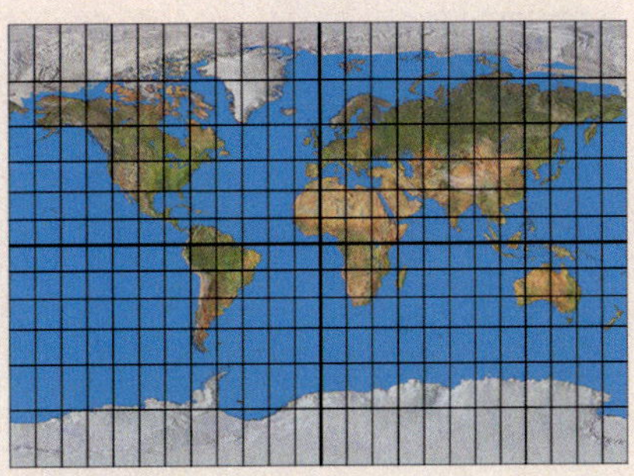

Mercator projection

ACTIVITIES

20. Correct the information.

a. Photographs taken by satellites are used in photo interpretation.

b. GIS is the science of obtaining information about the Earth's surface.

c. It is easy to represent the Earth accurately on a map.

d. Conic projection is mainly used to represent the whole planet.

21. What differences can you see between the cylindrical map shown and the map using the Peters projection? Explain them.

Discovery techniques

INTERPRETING A MAP

What are maps?

The **aim** of geography is to describe and analyse everything that occurs on the surface of the Earth.

To do this, geographers use maps. Maps are basic instruments that help them to describe and interpret the **phenomena** on the Earth's surface. Cartographers are the people who create maps. There are different types of maps depending on the area the cartographers want to display and the type of information they want to show.

They can be classified according to the area they represent:

- Maps of the Earth or **world maps**, which represent the entire surface of the planet.
- Maps of **large areas**, such as those that represent hemispheres or continents.
- **Specific** or small-area maps, which represent the surface of a country, an autonomous community, a province or a region.

Relief map of the world

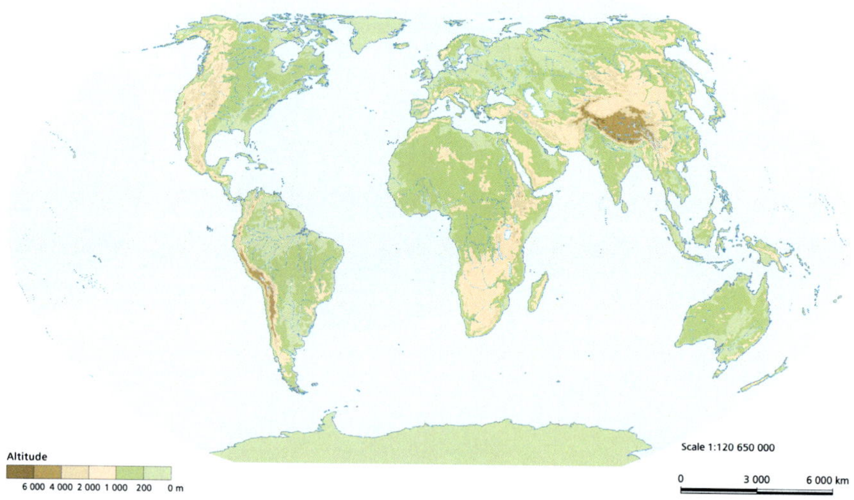

How are maps interpreted?

We use a scale and a key to help us interpret maps.

Scale

The scale of the map helps us to understand the size of the area represented.

The scale is the proportion between the real space represented and its representation on the map.

Small scales are used for large areas, such as the world and the continents. Larger scales are used to represent smaller areas, such as provinces and districts.

There are two types of scales:

- **A fractional scale.** This expresses the real distance as a **ratio** or fraction.

A 1:250 000 scale tells us that 1 cm on the map is equivalent to 250 000 cm (2.5 km) of the area represented.

- **A graphic scale.** This is a line with numbered segments. The numbers on the line indicate the real distance each segment represents on the map.

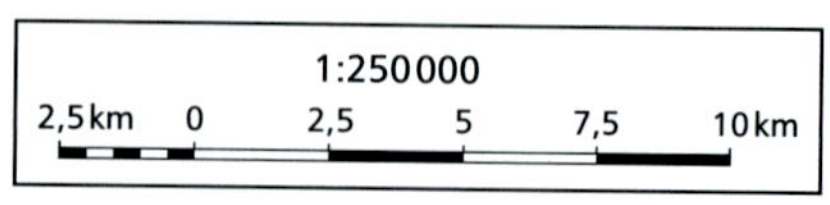

Key

Maps can provide a wide range of information. This information is indicated in the key.

The key is a group of conventional map symbols with an explanation of each symbol that gives us more information about the area represented.

> What information does a map include to help us interpret it?

What types of maps are there?

According to the information represented there are:

- **Topographic maps.** They are a detailed description of a place or region that show natural elements and changes made by humans.

  The places with the same height are linked with lines called **level curves.** The closer the level curves are, the **steeper** the incline in that area.

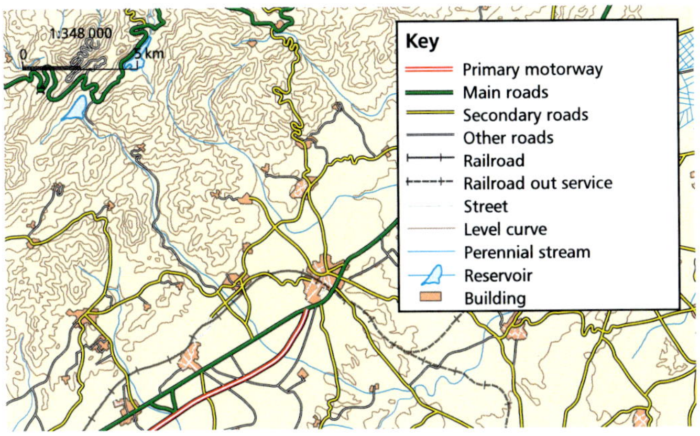

- **Thematic maps.** They show the distribution of a feature in the territory through information such as arrows, colours, lines, graphs, etc. This information is explained in the key.

  There are several types of thematic maps (geographical, historical, economic, road, population, etc.).

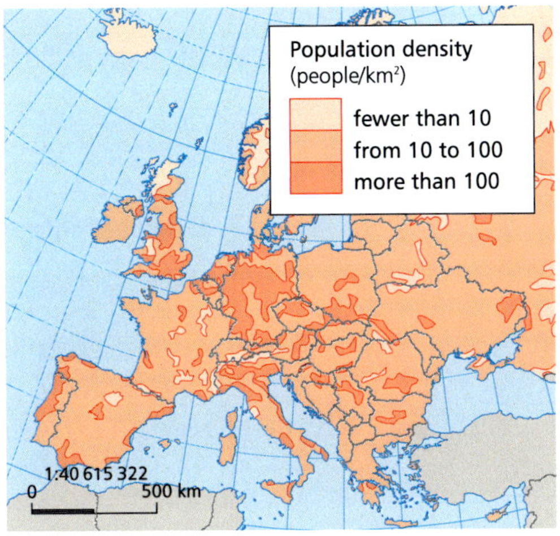

- **Physical maps.** They show geographical coordinates (parallels and meridians) and landforms.

  Different colours are used to represent altitude.

PRACTISE WHAT YOU'VE LEARNT

1. Find a map of Spain in an atlas. Use a ruler and find out the approximate distances between Cabo de Creus and Cabo de la Noa, and between Cabo de Finisterre and the Strait of Gibraltar.
2. If the scale of a map is 1:500 000, how many kilometres are the following distances equal to: 47.73 cm and 105 cm?
3. Use an atlas or the Internet to find a population density map of Spain's provinces. Look at the key and answer these questions:
   - Which provinces are most heavily populated?
   - What is the population density for the province of Cadiz?
   - Name three of the provinces with the lowest population density.

Revision activities

1 Rewrite the sentences in your notebooks. Replace 'They' with the celestial body 'they' is referring to.

a. They are small pieces of rock and **debris** that sometimes fall to the Earth.
b. They are huge and they emit light and heat.
c. They have a nucleus of ice or rocks and a gaseous tail.
d. They orbit the closest planet and they do not emit light or heat.
e. They are made of rock and most of them orbit the Sun.
f. They orbit the closest star and they do not emit light or heat.

2 Why is the Earth a habitable planet? Copy and complete the text.

The (a) ______________ on Earth are not (b) ______________ . On other planets they can (c) ______________ hundreds of degrees above or below zero. In addition, the Earth is protected from solar radiation by the (d) ______________ . This is made up of (e) ______________ . The other element essential to life on Earth is (f) ______________ , which covers (g) ______________ of the planet.

3 Define *rotation* and *revolution*. Explain the effects of these movements.

4 What is the shape of the orbit drawn by the Earth in its revolution movement around the Sun? Do you think this shape influences the changing of the seasons? Why?

5 Search for the definition of *solstice* and *equinox* on the Internet. Look carefully at the image below and match the phases of the diagram (A to D) to the following events:

- spring equinox
- autumn equinox
- summer solstice
- winter solstice

According to the date in the diagram, when will each of these events occur?

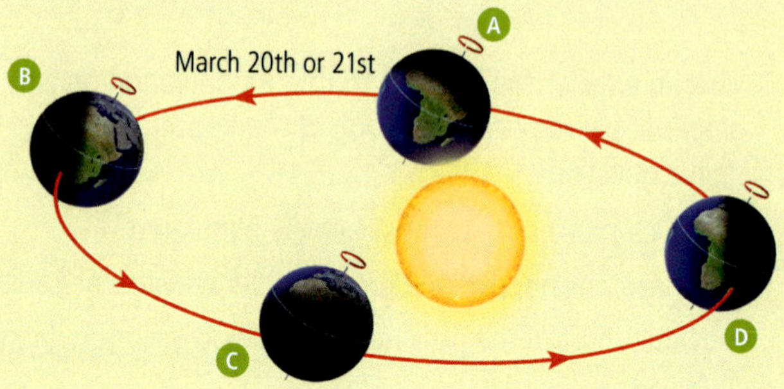

6 Match the sentence halves. Write the completed sentences in your notebook.

1. The seasons are the result of …
2. It is winter in the Northern hemisphere when …
3. It is spring or autumn when …
4. It is summer in the Northern hemisphere when …

a. the Sun's rays fall on the Southern hemisphere.
b. the Sun's rays fall on the Northern hemisphere.
c. the tilt of the Earth and its orbit round the Sun.
d. the Sun's rays fall on the Equator.

7 Why are summers not as hot in the poles as they are in other regions of the planet?

8 What area of the Earth experiences the most differences between summer and winter? Explain your answer.

9 In our calendar, every four years February has an extra day. Why do you think this is?

10 Use the Internet. Find out what the International Dateline is and why and how it moved in 1995. Explain your findings to the class.

11 Define the following concepts: Solar System, atmosphere, time zones, Prime Meridian.

12 Use an atlas and look at the map on page 12.

Can you solve the following problems? Explain your answers.

a. It's 2 p.m. here in Ottawa. My friend in London gets home from school at 4 p.m. Is it a good time to phone her?
b. It's 10 p.m. here in London. I don't know whether to phone my friend in Nairobi. Do you think it's a good idea?
c. It's 12:00 in Moscow. Moscow's in Russia. Vladivostock is in Russia too. But it's 22:00 in Vladivostock. I really don't understand it.
d. My father's flying from London to Los Angeles. The flight takes 11 hours and 15 minutes. He left London at 10:25 and he gets to Los Angeles at 14:40. It seems impossible to me!

13 Think of a foreign city you would like to visit. Find out:

a. how long it would take you to fly there.
b. the time difference between your city and the one you want to visit.

14 Look at the map in the centre of this page. Find the cities with the following geographic coordinates:

- 40° 40′ N y 73° 56′ W
- 35° 41′ N y 139° 46′ E
- 34° 35′ S y 58° 22′ W
- 35° 18′ S y 149° 08′ E

15 What are the main cartographic tools? Briefly explain how to get information from each one of them.

18 Complete the table.

Type of map projection	Most used for maps of …	Problems
Conic		
Plane		Mainly only used for polar regions
	the whole planet	

19 Compare a Mercator map projection with a Peters one. Which one do you think represents reality better? Explain your answer.

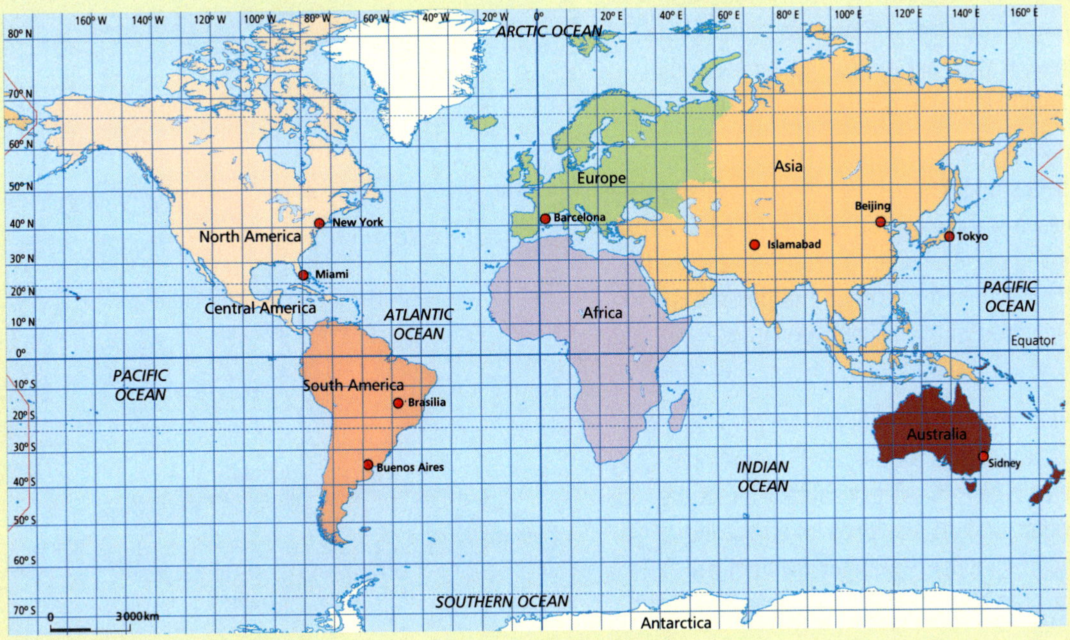

16 Make sentences using all the words given.

a. Photo interpretation / photographs / Earth / aeroplanes

b. Remote sensing / information / cameras / aeroplanes / satellites

c. geographic information system / computer system / geographic data

17 Look at the photo. Write a short paragraph about what you think it represents.

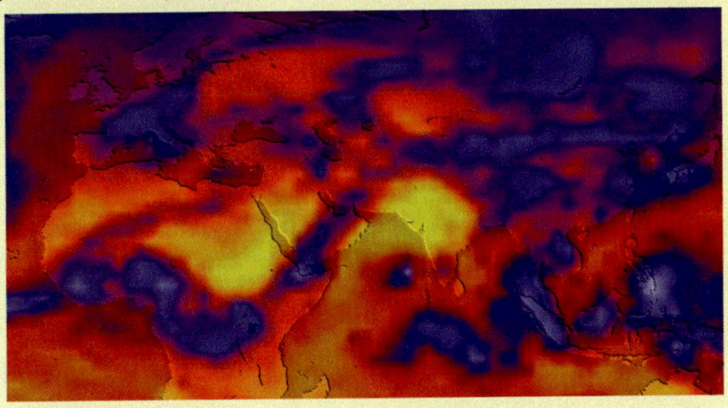

20 Define the following concepts: *geographical coordinates, map projection, scale of a map.*

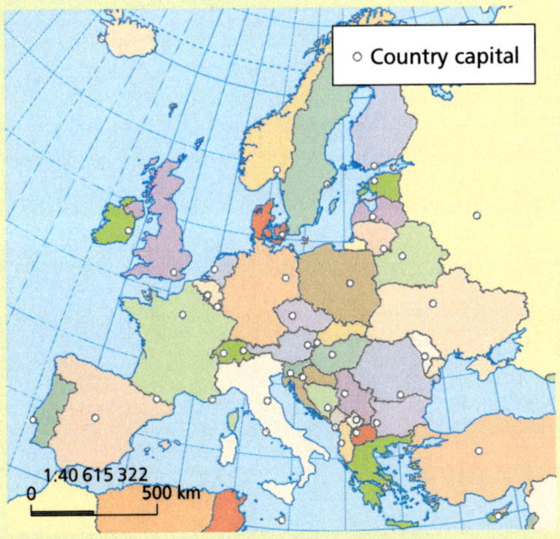

21 Look at the map and answer the questions:

a. What type of map is it?

b. What type of information does it contain?

Read and think

HOW DOES A GPS RECEIVER WORK?

In the past, if people didn't know the way to a place, they used a map. Today, many people no longer use maps because they have a GPS, or a Sat Nav, as it is usually called in the United Kingdom.

But what exactly is GPS? GPS stands for Global Positioning System. It is a satellite navigation system which provides information about location and time anywhere on the Earth. The system works by using a group of between twenty and thirty satellites. The navigation system needs a direct line of sight to at least four satellites.

So what does it do? The GPS receiver calculates its position by timing the signals sent by the GPS satellites. The satellites transmit messages. These messages include the time the message was transmitted and the position of the satellite when the message was transmitted.

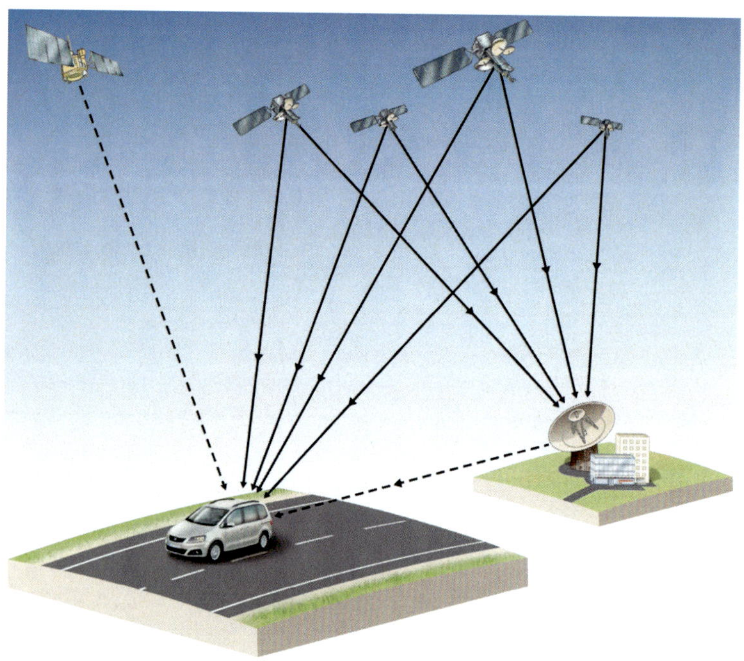

With the messages it receives, the receiver calculates how long the message took to arrive and also calculates the distance to each satellite using the speed of light. These distances and the location of the satellites are used to work out the position of the receiver. This position is then shown, sometimes with a map or with latitude and longitude.

Although GPS was originally used for military purposes, it has many applications in everyday life. It is, for example, essential for the emergency services to quickly locate the position of accidents or disasters. It has also made life much easier for cartographers – using GPS and other technologies, they can base their maps accurately on the **terrain**.

ANSWER THE QUESTIONS

1. What does 'GPS' stand for?
2. What do you think 'Sat Nav' is short for?
3. How many satellites are there in a GPS system?
4. What does your GPS receiver calculate?
5. How is a GPS receiver's position shown?
6. Why is GPS useful to the emergency services?
7. There is a service called GPS Tour. What do you think this is? Discuss your ideas with a partner. Then use the Internet to check your answers.
8. Does anyone you know have a GPS on their phone? Write a paragraph explaining what they use it for.

Work it out

CONCEPT MAP

Use the words in the word cloud to create your own unit map in your notebook.
Write any connecting texts you need.

asteroids Solar System planets Earth
space meteorites water latitude location
habitable meridians universe
geographic coordinates satellites celestial bodies
orientation comets parallels
longitude temperature stars atmosphere

SELF-ASSESSMENT

Carry out a self-assessment of what you have learnt in this unit. Choose one answer for each question and then check your answers.

1. Celestial bodies are grouped into …
   a. systems
   b. constellations
   c. galaxies

2. The Milky Way is in the shape of a …
   a. circle
   b. spiral
   c. geoid

3. There is no life on Mercury because …
   a. it is too hot there.
   b. it is not a planet.
   c. it is too far from the Sun.

4. The Earth's axial tilt is …
   a. 23° 27'.
   b. 22° 27'.
   c. 24° 27'.

5. What is the main aim of geography?
   a. To study geographical space.
   b. To study the elements that affect geographical space.
   c. Both A and B.

6. To locate a point on the Earth's surface, we need to use …
   a. parallels and meridians.
   b. altitude and parallels.
   c. altitude and meridians.

7. The Equator is …
   a. the centre of the Earth.
   b. the 0° meridian.
   c. the 0° parallel.

8. The type of projection most commonly used to show the whole planet is …
   a. cylindrical
   b. conic
   c. plane

9. The techniques most commonly used to represent the Earth's surface are …
   a. photo interpretation.
   b. remote sensing.
   c. both A and B.

10. The key to a map …
    a. helps us find a location.
    b. gives us more information.
    c. tells us real distances.

02 Geosphere: Relief and landforms

<< LOOKING BACK

- What do we find deep inside the Earth?
- Approximately what percentage of the Earth is covered by water?
- How can we represent the Earth?
- What types of maps are most suitable for representing the form of the Earth's surface?

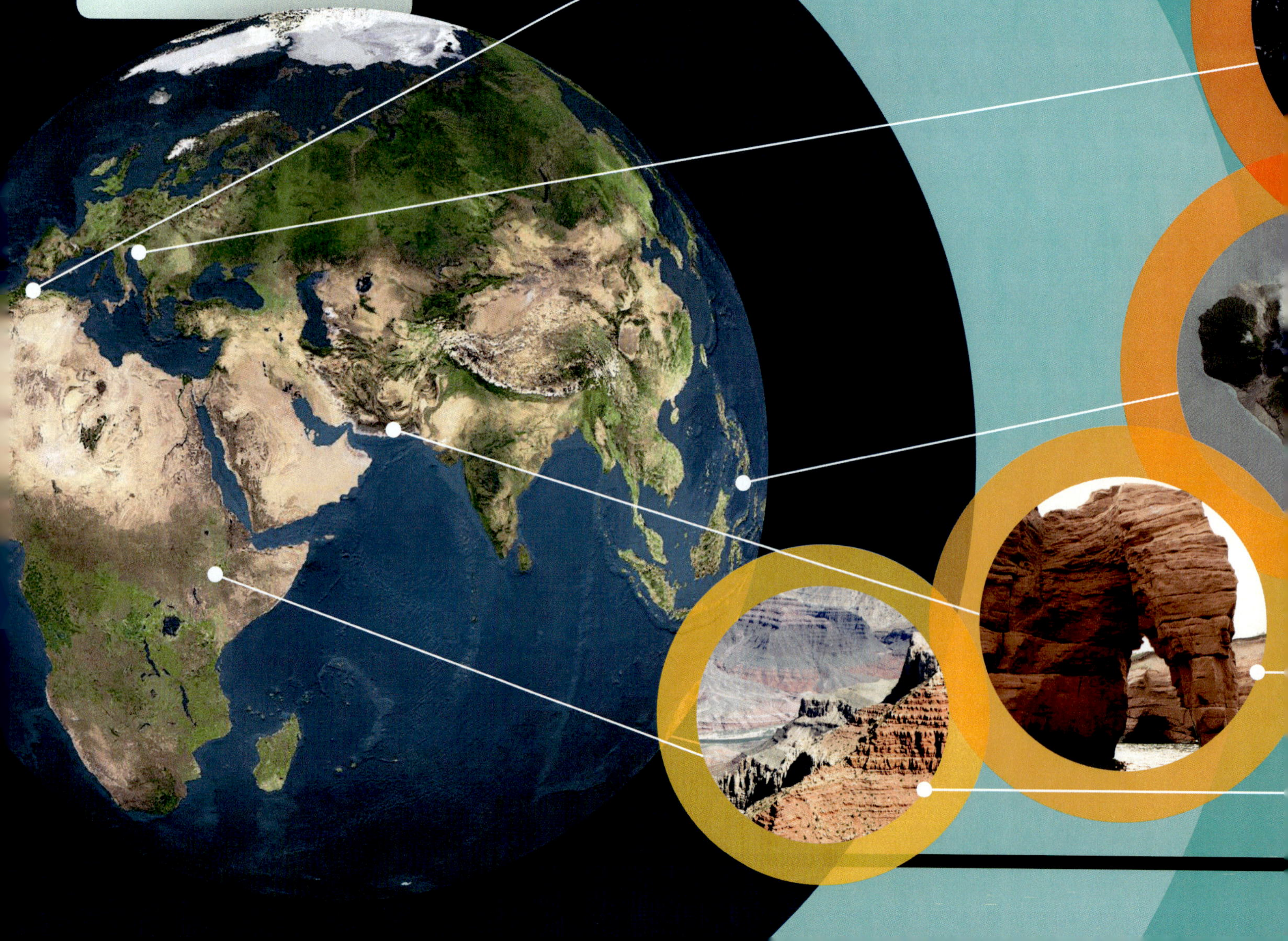

From Pangaea to today's continents

Geologists believe that about 350 million years ago there was only one big continent. They decided to call it Pangaea. It was surrounded by one big ocean, which they called Panthalassa.

More recently, 150 million years ago, the huge continent **split into** two land masses, which were given the names of Laurasia and Gondwana. These two land masses then split again and again until the continents were distributed as we know today. There is substantial evidence to suggest that the continents were once joined together. For example, similar plant and animal fossils have been found near the coast in countries on different continents, like in Brazil and South Africa.

Today **geophysicists** believe that tectonic plates are responsible for the movement and separation of the land masses.

- What are the continents that we know today?
- In your opinion, in what way could tectonic plates cause the separation of land masses?

LOOKING FORWARD >>

- What is the external layer of the geosphere called?
- What is the process of mountain formation called?
- What types of continental landforms are there?
- How much of the Earth's surface is taken up by land?
- What types of chart or graph are used to express geographical data?

1 The internal structure of the Earth

➲ What is the external layer of the geosphere called?

The geosphere is the solid part of the Earth. It is made up of rocks and other solid elements.

1.1 The geosphere

The geosphere is divided into three different **layers**:

CRUST

It is the outermost, thinnest layer of the Earth. It is made up of rocks and it is divided into:

- Oceanic crust
- Continental crust

The crust measures between 6 and 70 km. It represents 1% of the planet's volume.

MANTLE

It is the layer between the crust and the core. It is the largest layer and contains **magma**. Magma is a mixture of molten and semi-molten rock that is extremely hot. When it is ejected by a volcano, magma is called **lava**.

The mantle is divided into two parts: the upper mantle and the lower mantle. It represents 84% of the planet's volume.

CORE

It is the innermost layer. It is also the layer we know the least about. Scientists believe it is made up of very heavy minerals such as iron and nickel, which can be in a viscous or solid state.

The core lies at a depth of between 2 900 and 6 370 km. It represents 15% of the planet's volume.

BIG THINKER

Alfred Wegener, a German scientist, proposed the theory of continental drift: the idea that the Earth's continents move. Despite the evidence he presented, his theory was initially rejected by most other scientists. When the theory of plate tectonics was recognised as being correct in the 1960s, geologists finally accepted Wegener's continental drift theory and his concept of Pangaea.

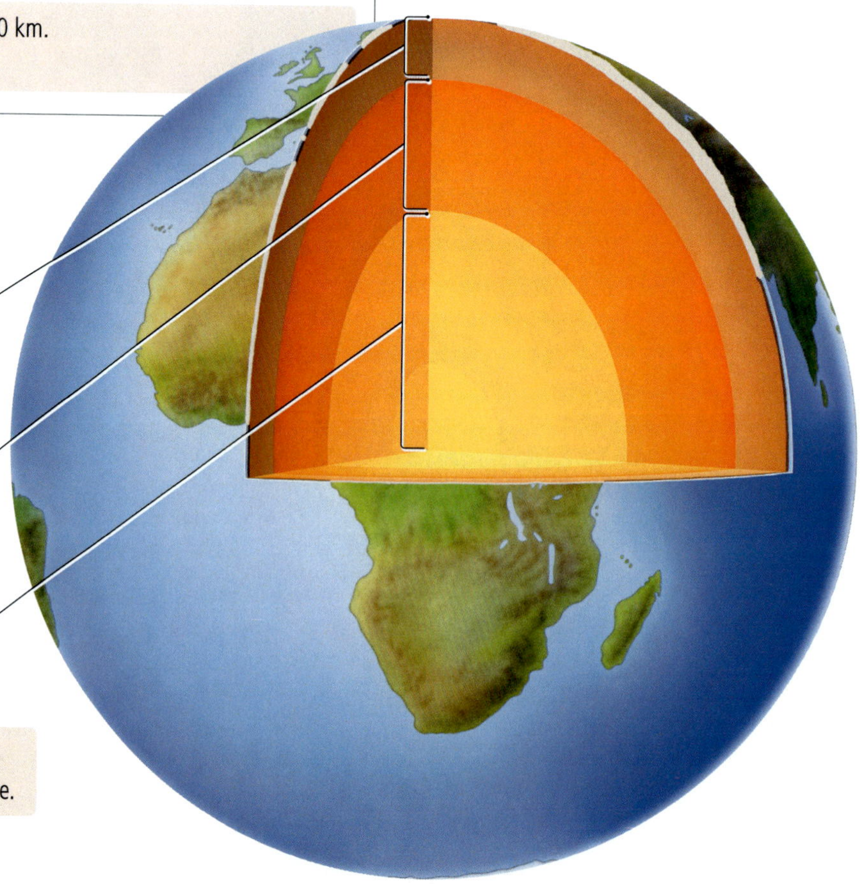

1.2 Plate tectonics

The surface of the Earth is in a state of constant motion and evolution due to the planet's internal forces. These changes occur in the **lithosphere**, which is formed by the crust and the upper mantle. The scientific study of the movements and changes of the lithosphere is called plate tectonics.

TECTONIC PLATES

The lithosphere is divided into **tectonic plates**, which are blocks that float on top of the molten materials in the mantle. There are plates under the ocean, called **oceanic plates**, and plates under the continents, called **continental plates**.

The movement of the tectonic plates is constant and very slow. There are two basic movements: collision and separation.

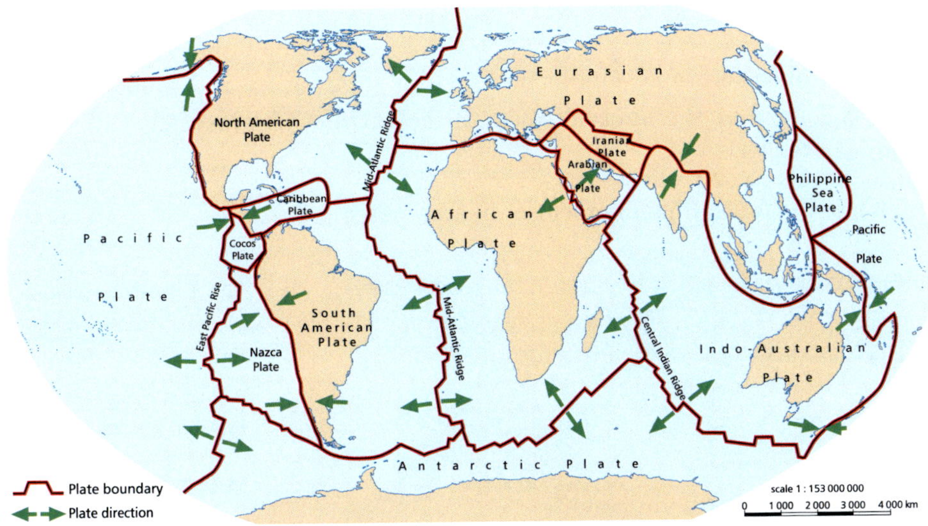

The tectonic plates

Collision

When two plates collide, it can result in:

- The formation of a very unstable area known as a **fault**, which is a break in the Earth's crust where **earthquakes** are common.
- Mountain formation, when the edges of the plates **fold** and rise. If the thinner edge is buried under the thicker one, it causes part of the crust to disappear.

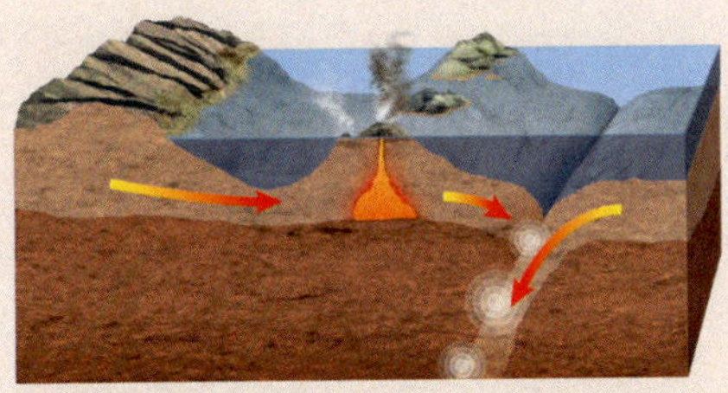
Collision can cause land to disappear.

Separation

When two plates separate, this creates a **fissure** where the magma from inside the Earth comes up to the surface. When lava cools, it forms a new layer of crust called a **ridge**, or mountain range.

Separation can produce new land.

ACTIVITIES

1. Read the definitions and identify the word.
   a. This forms the largest part of the Earth.
   b. This is a thin layer of the Earth, made of rocks.
   c. This is the centre of the Earth.
   d. This part of the mantle is situated below the lithosphere.
   e. This is the thickest layer inside the Earth.
2. Look at the map of the tectonic plates.
   a. Which plates are the largest? Are they oceanic or continental?
   b. How many plates are there in total?
3. Where do you think most volcanoes are located in relation to the tectonic plates? Support your opinion with evidence from a reliable source.

2 Relief formation

What is the process of mountain formation called?

The Earth's relief consists of the natural forms and features that make up the surface of the planet. They are formed by plate tectonics and the action of external agents which change and shape them.

2.1 Internal forces

The formation of elevated landforms, such as mountains and mountain ranges, is caused by the internal forces of the Earth. This process is called **orogenesis**.

We can identify four different processes in orogenesis:

Volcanic mountain formation occurs when two tectonic plates separate, creating a ridge. Magma erupts from the volcano. This **lava** cools and solidifies, forming mountain ranges and volcanic cones.

Volcanic mountain formation

Fault blocks occur when forces act on blocks of hard materials which cannot fold. These forces produce earthquakes, which break up the blocks. This forms a relief made of raised and lowered blocks.

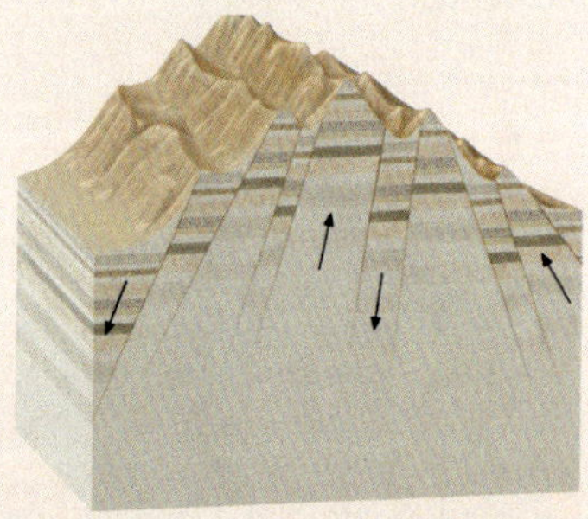

Fault-block mountain formation

Folding occurs when two tectonic plates with edges made of relatively soft materials collide. The edges of the plates fold and rise, creating large mountains.

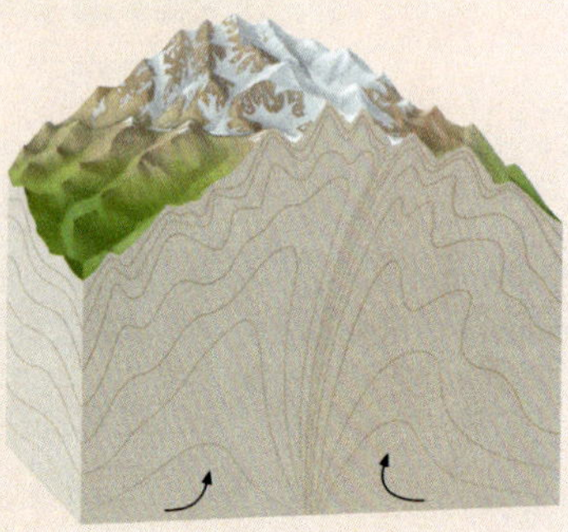

Mountain formation by folding

Folding and subduction occur when a thinner oceanic plate and a thicker continental plate collide, and the oceanic plate sinks forming a trench. The edge of the continental plate folds and rises, forming a mountain range.

Mountain formation by folding and subduction

2.2 External agents

Elevated landforms are modified by the action of **external agents**: water, wind and living beings.

External agents shape the Earth's relief through the interaction of three **geological processes**:

- **Erosion** is the disintegration of landforms by the external agents.
- **Transportation** is the movement of the eroded materials.
- **Deposition** is when the transported materials are deposited in areas of low relief.

ACTIVITIES

4. Which two factors are responsible for shaping the Earth's relief?
5. Define the concept of orogenesis.

2.3 Types of erosion and deposition

Fluvial erosion is caused by rivers. The force of the water erodes the landforms, and deposits the sediment in lower areas.

Glacial erosion is caused by glaciers. Glaciers are masses of ice that move very slowly. They erode the surface and deposit sediment, forming **moraines**.

Coastal erosion is caused by the movement of the sea, such as waves, tides and currents. The sea shapes the coasts, forming cliffs or depositing materials on the beaches.

Wind erosion is caused by particles carried by the wind. These particles erode elevated landforms when they hit them. The sediment transported by the wind is then deposited, forming piles of sand or **dunes**.

Freezing and thawing erosion is caused by water penetrating the cracks on rocky surfaces. When the water freezes, its volume increases producing bigger cracks in the earth and rocks.

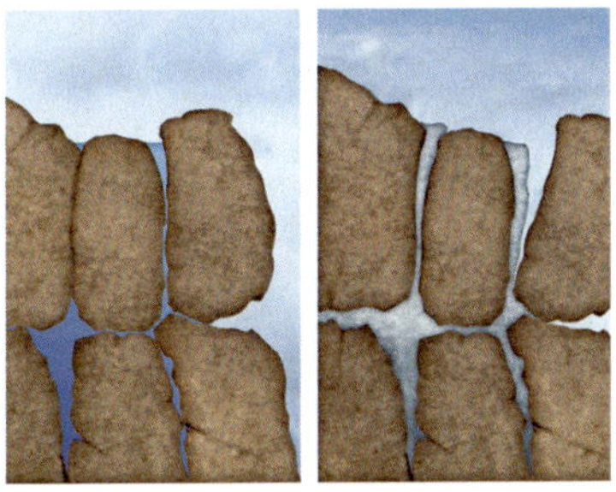

Biological erosion is caused by living things. For example, plants break the soil with their roots and animals erode the soil when they build their **dens**.

HUMAN ACTIVITY

Nowadays, the most significant agents in shaping the Earth's surface are humans. Through the use of technology and heavy machinery, we shape the Earth according to our needs. We flatten areas for agricultural purposes, and create artificial islands, hills, and plateaus.

Human activity also has a major influence on erosion. The felling of trees is the number-one cause of vegetation loss. Without vegetation, Earth's surface has very little protection against erosion caused by wind and water.

ACTIVITIES

6. Name the external agents responsible for relief formation. Explain how they change the shape of the landscape.
7. External agents can be divided into three distinct geological processes. What are they?

3 Types of relief

The Earth's surface is made up of tectonic plates that are constantly in motion as they collide or slide past each other. The collisions can cause earthquakes or volcanic eruptions. Relief is the result of plate tectonics and the shaping of the Earth's surface by external agents i.e. water, wind and living things.

There are three main types of relief: **continental**, **coastal** and **ocean**.

3.1 Continental relief

Landforms are natural physical features of the Earth's surface. Continental relief landforms can be divided into four main types: plateaus, plains, valleys, and mountains.

PLATEAUS

These are flat or gently **undulating** areas located at an average altitude of about 650 m above sea level. On plateaus, erosion leaves the hardest rocks exposed.

High plateaus are located between major mountain ranges at altitudes above to 3 000 m.

PLAINS

These are flat areas located at altitudes below 150 m. The materials they are made up of are the result of transportation and deposition processes. Plains are often fertile areas that are good for agriculture.

DID YOU KNOW?

The Altiplano-Puna plateau in the Andes is the second highest in the world after the Tibetan plateau. It is about 1 800 km long and 350 - 400 km wide. The largest part of the plateau is in Peru and Bolivia. There are several cities there, including La Paz, the capital of Bolivia.

What types of continental landforms are there?

ALTITUDE AND HEIGHT

Altitude is the height of a mountain peak above sea level. Mount Everest is the mountain with the highest altitude in the world: 8 848 metres.

Height is the distance between the base of a mountain and its peak. The Mauna Loa volcano, on the island of Hawaii, is the world's highest mountain. Its base is under the ocean, at 5 500 metres below sea level. The volcano measures 9 767 metres from its base to its peak.

MOUNTAINS

These are the highest landforms. They have steep slopes and rugged terrain. The average height of a mountain is between 1 000 and 3 500 metres above sea level. Very high mountains are rare. Depending on their height, structure and size, mountains are classified as independent mountains or mountain ranges.

VALLEYS

These are sunken areas between mountains or plateaus. They usually have a river running through them. When river valleys are very large, they are called depressions or basins.

3.2 Coastal relief

Coastal relief is located in areas where the emerging land is in contact with the sea.

- If the continental area is flat and has a low altitude, it forms flat, low coasts dominated by **beaches**.
- If the continental area is mountainous, it forms high coasts with slopes and **cliffs**.

Coastal relief is made up of several landforms:

- **Peninsulas** are areas of land connected to the mainland and surrounded by water on three sides.
- **Capes** are pieces of land which extend into the sea. If the cape is small, it is called a **point**.
- **Gulfs** are areas of the sea surrounded by land except on one side. If a gulf is small, it is called a **bay**.
- **Inlets** are areas where the sea floods into a deep and narrow valley. Inlets are called ***fjords*** when they form in glacial valleys. Inlets are a typical feature of the Galician coastline in the north west of Spain, where they are called ***rías***.
- **Islands** are pieces of land surrounded by water on all sides. An **archipelago** is a group of islands.

3.3 Ocean relief

Ocean relief landforms are little known because they are located at great depths. However, the landforms at the bottom of the sea are as varied as those on the Earth's surface. There are five major types of landform:

Continental shelves are large, flat areas which extend from the coast and reach a depth of around 300 m.

Ocean ridges are very high underwater mountain ranges located in the middle of the oceans. Their highest areas may emerge from the water, creating islands or archipelagos.

Continental slopes are steep slopes that connect continental shelves with ocean basins.

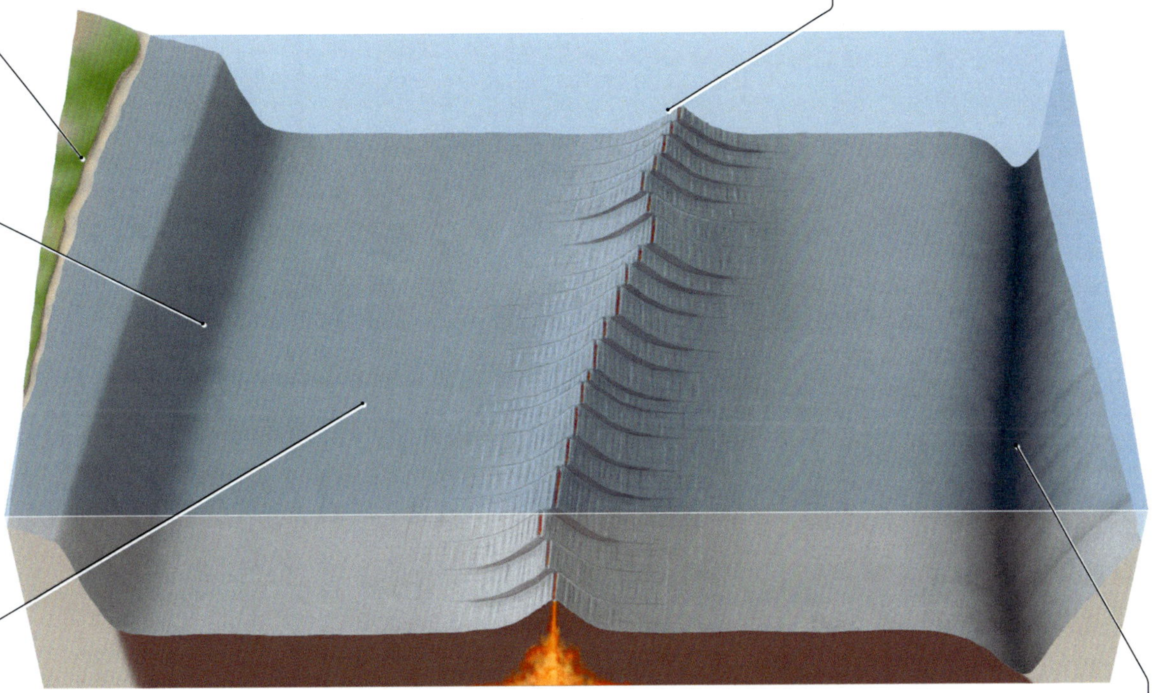

Ocean basins are large plains at a depth of between 3 000 and 6 000 m that cover most of the bottom of the sea. Sometimes, volcanic islands emerge from them. Ocean basins are also called abyssal plains.

Ocean trenches are narrow crevices located along the edges of ocean basins. They are some of the deepest areas of the planet.

ACTIVITIES

8. In which three categories do we divide the Earth's relief into?
9. Read the definitions and decide which continental landforms each one is describing.
   a. These are the highest landforms. They have steep slopes.
   b. These are areas between mountains.
   c. These are low areas which have been formed by transportation and deposition.
   d. These are very high, flat areas between mountains.
10. Complete the sentences.
    a. A ... is land which is surrounded by water on three sides.
    b. An ... is a group of islands.
    c. A ... is land which extends into the sea.
    d. A ... is a long narrow inlet with steep sides.
    e. A ... is a small gulf.
11. Correct the information in your notebook.
    a. Continental shelves are found in the middle of the ocean.
    b. Continental slopes are next to ocean trenches.
    c. Ocean ridges are found near the coast.
    d. Abyssal plains are very steep.

4 The Earth's continents

There are two main types of area on Earth: **marine and oceanic waters**, which make up most of the surface, and **emergent landmasses**, which account for only a third of the Earth's surface.

Most emergent landmasses are parts of **continents**, which are defined as huge expanses of land surrounded by marine waters.

In addition to the continents, there are **islands**, which are also emergent landmasses, but of a smaller size.

AMERICA

The American continent has an elongated shape that runs from north to south. If you look at it, you can see two **subcontinents**: the combined areas of North and Central America, and South America. America has a total area of approximately 42 091 000 km². To the north, it is bordered by the Arctic Ocean, to the east by the Atlantic, to the south by the Southern Ocean (or Antarctic Ocean), and to the west by the Pacific, where it is divided from the Asian continent by the Bering Strait.

America's islands and archipelagos are mostly located in the Atlantic Ocean. These include Caribbean islands such as Cuba and Hispaniola (home to the Dominican Republic and Haiti), and the archipelagos off the Canadian coast.

In the English-speaking world, North America and South America are considered separate continents. That means that many people argue there are seven continents, not six!

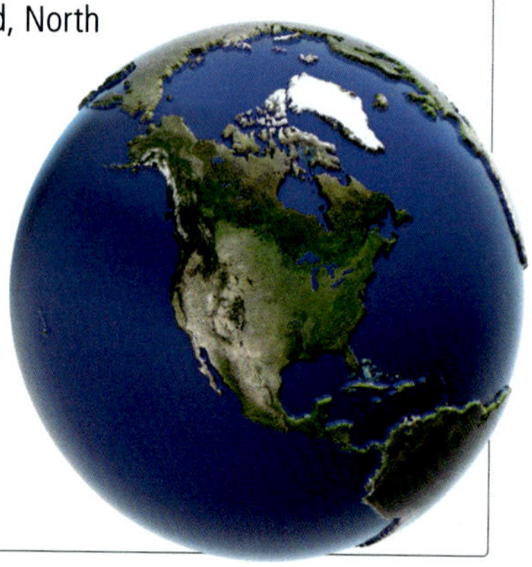

ANTARCTICA

The Antarctic continent has an area of approximately 13 177 000 km². It is separated from South America by the Drake Passage.

This continent is located inside the Antarctic Circle, which is why almost all of it is covered in ice. Geographical studies have shown that it consists of numerous islands and a large continental landmass.

How much of the Earth's surface is taken up by land?

The continents are: **Asia**, **Africa**, **America**, **Europe**, **Antarctica** and **Oceania.** This division into continents is not strictly physical because, from a geographical perspective, Europe and Asia form a single unit, called Eurasia. However, for cultural and political reasons, they are regarded as independent continents.

Furthermore, most of the continents are in the Northern hemisphere in the eastern part. Only the American continent is located in the Western hemisphere.

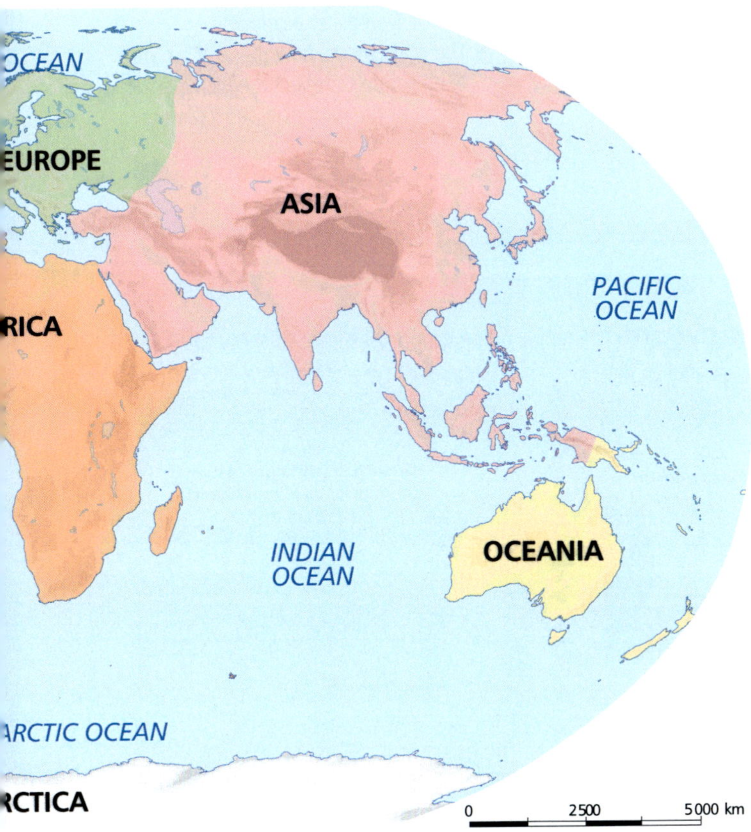

EUROPE

Europe is the fifth largest continent, with an area of 10 522 000 km^2.

It is bordered by the Atlantic Ocean, the Arctic Ocean and the Mediterranean Sea, which separates it from Africa, as well as by the Ural Mountains, which separate it from Asia.

European islands in the Atlantic Ocean, such as the British Isles, are fairly large.

There are several islands in the Mediterranean. Among these, Sicily and Sardinia are the largest.

ASIA

The Asian continent is the largest landmass in the world, having an area of approximately 44 308 000 km^2.

The main archipelagos are located in the eastern and southeastern parts of the continent. The largest ones form the countries of Japan, the Philippines and Indonesia.

Islands in the Malay Archipelago form parts of countries that, politically speaking, are considered to be from two different continents, i.e. Asia and Oceania.

OCEANIA

Oceania is the smallest continent, with an area of about 8 946 000 km^2.

It is made up of different islands, the largest of which is Australia. A group of medium-sized islands, such as New Guinea, New Zealand and Tasmania, form part of this continent, as do a large number of archipelagos and thousands of small islands in the Melanesian, Polynesian and Micronesian groups.

Some authorities consider Australia to be a continent, rather than an island.

AFRICA

The African continent has an area of approximately 30 310 000 km^2.

Its islands are extremely limited in number. The island of Madagascar and small archipelagos, such as the Canary Islands and the Seychelles, are some of the most important.

Madagascar, with an area of 600 000 km^2, is the fourth largest island in the world.

Discovery techniques

GEOGRAPHICAL GRAPHS AND CHARTS

What are graphs and charts?

One of the most useful tools for a geographer is statistical data about a particular geographical phenomenon. This could be the height of a range of mountains or the annual temperature in a given place.

Numerical data of this kind can be organised in statistical tables. If you present the information in these tables **pictorially** by means of coordinate axes and different shapes such as bars, lines, circles, etc, you have a useful tool called a chart or graph. Basically, a graph is a pictorial representation of a set of numerical data. The items of data presented in a graph are called variables.

Charts enable us to analyse or compare data quickly and visually. They also allow us to study how a phenomenon changes over time.

THE ELEMENTS OF A GRAPH OR CHART

All graphs have certain features in common which make it easier to interpret them.

- The title must stand out and present the information in a clear and concrete way.
- The key explains the data through the use of symbols and colours.
- The scale shows how the axes have been set up to reflect the incremental shape of the data from the variables.

Types of graphs and charts

PIE CHART

A pie chart is a circle divided into sections. The size of each section is proportional to the value it represents.

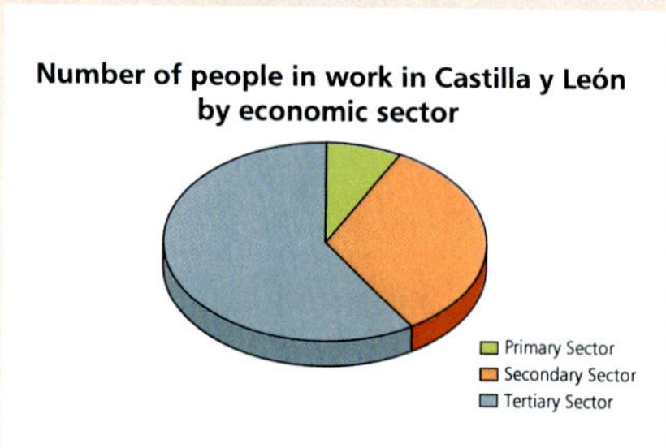

The circle as a whole represents 100% of the variables. Each sector represents one variable as a smaller percentage of the total.

BAR CHART

A bar chart uses rectangular bars. The length of the bars is proportional to the values they represent.

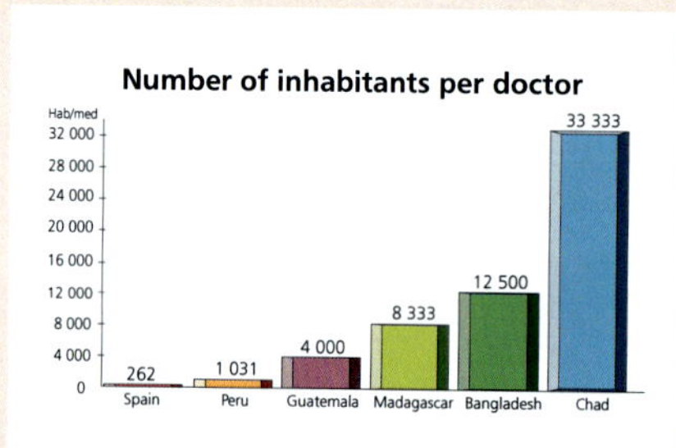

The bars can also be positioned vertically, in which case it is known as a **column chart**.

LINE GRAPH

A line graph uses lines to show the change over time of one or more different phenomena.

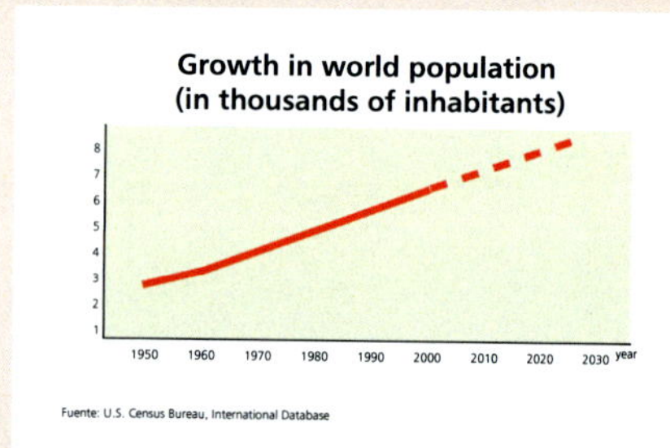

The horizontal axis represents different times and the vertical axis shows the value of the variable at each time. The recorded values are joined together with a line.

POPULATIONPYRAMID

A population pyramid is a double graph consisting of bars which represent the distribution of the population in groups according to age and **gender**.

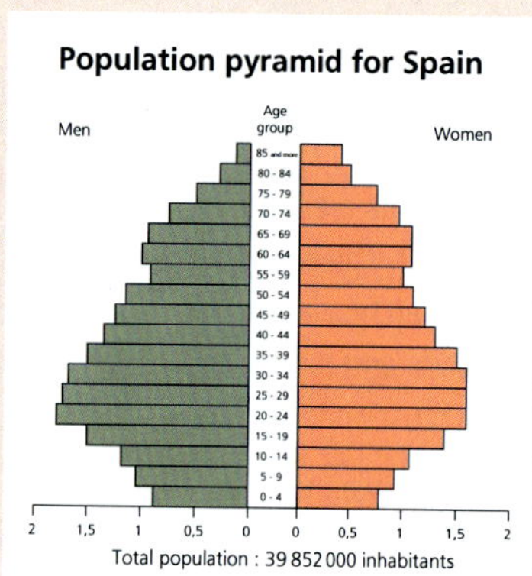

CLIMOGRAPH

A climograph is a mixed type of graph consisting of both bars and lines. It presents the most representative climatic data for a particular place.

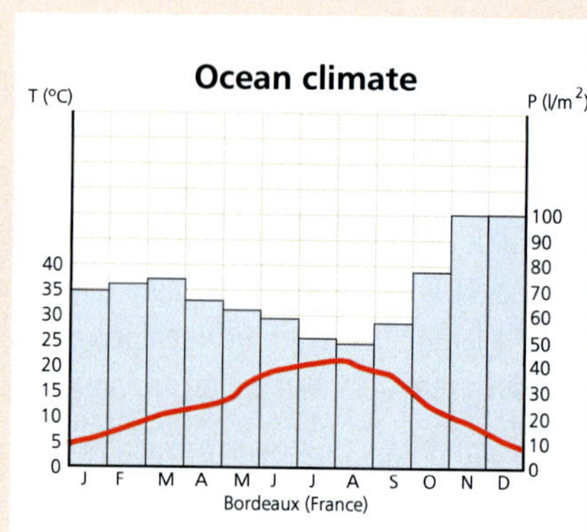

What types of chart or graph are used to express geographical data?

How to create a pie chart

1 Collect data about a particular topic. In this case, we're going to use the sizes of the oceans.

Oceans	Approximate size (in 1 000s of km²)
Antarctic	20 300
Arctic	14 000
Atlantic	76 800
Indian	68 600
Pacific	155 600
TOTAL suface covered by oceans	335 300

2 Next, change this numerical data into percentages. To do this, use the following formula:

$$\text{Data expressed as a percentage} = \frac{\text{Numerical data}}{\text{Total}} \times 100$$

For example, in the case of the Antarctic Ocean, it would be:

$$(20\,300 / 335\,300) \times 100 = 6.05\%$$

3 Perform this calculation on all the items of data which you want to show in your graph. The resulting figures can be rounded up or down.

Oceans	Percentage of total	
Antarctic	6.05%	6%
Arctic	4.18%	4%
Atlantic	22.90%	23%
Indian	20.46%	20%
Pacific	46.41%	46%

4 Create the pie chart by using correspondingly sized slices of the pie to represent the various percentages.

First, draw a circle.

Then calculate the portion of the circumference that corresponds to each percentage, bearing in mind that the entire circumference corresponds to 360°. For example, in the case of the Antarctic Ocean, 5% is equivalent to 18° (360 × 5/100 = 18°) on the graph.

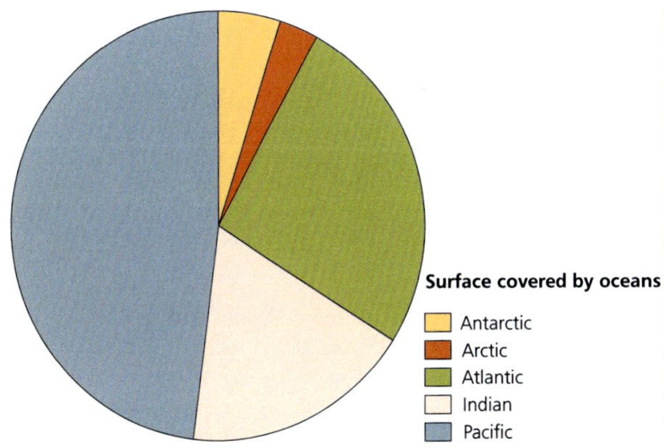

Use a **protractor** to help you enter the data in the circle. There will be a radius for each of the pieces of data we want to show. The radiuses delimit the circular segments that represent each item of data. Each segment should be coloured differently.

5 Finally, add the title, key and the percentage which each segment represents.

PRACTISE WHAT YOU'VE LEARNT

1. Say what type of graph you would use to represent the following types of data:
   - to compare the sizes of the largest islands in the world.
   - to show the changes in the ice caps of the Arctic Ocean over a period of 10 years.
   - to compare the surface area of the emergent landmasses in each hemisphere.
2. Look through the unit for data about the surface areas of the continents and present this information in a pie chart.

Revision activities

1. Look at the diagram on page 26 and answer the following questions:
   a. What is the lithosphere?
   b. What is magma?
   c. Which layer/s of the geosphere does the endosphere include?
   d. Which layer occupies the most volume? Which occupies the least?

2. Explain the difference between an 'ocean ridge' and an 'ocean trench'.

3. Look at the diagram below and answer the following questions:
   a. What theory does the image represent? Briefly explain the theory.
   b. Do you think the continents will remain in their current positions indefinitely? What will the continents be like in millions of years?

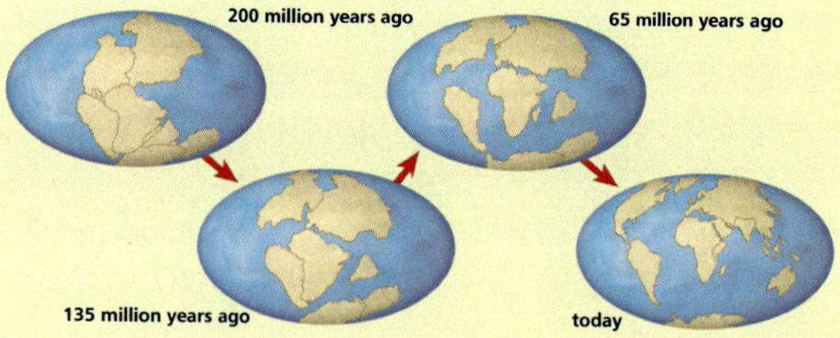

4. Why do you think water is the most active external agent in relief formation? Name the different types of erosion that water causes and match each type to one of the photos below.

5. How does wind contribute to erosion? Draw an example of the type of formations that can produce.

6. What role does temperature play in relief formation?

7. What does 'biological erosion' mean? What living organism has the biggest impact on the Earth's relief? Provide an example to justify your answer.

8. Explain why vegetation both causes and prevents erosion.

9. Copy and label the following illustration in your notebook.

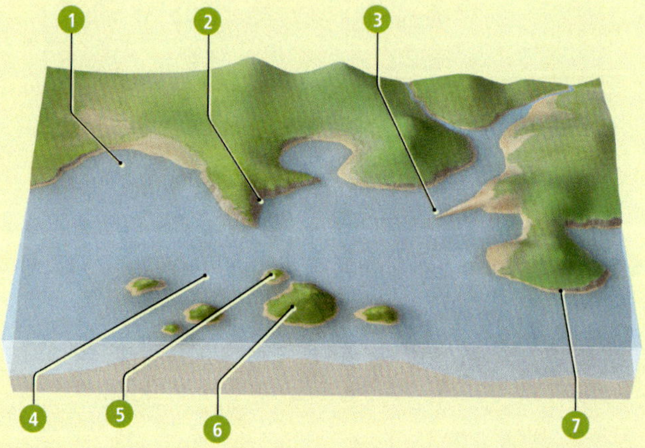

10. Explain the difference between altitude and height. Use the illustration to help you.

11. Define the following terms: lithosphere, tectonic plates, Pangaea, meseta, cape, peninsula, fjord, abyssal basin.

12. Name the main landforms in continental and coastal zones.

13. Explain what coastal zones are. What landforms would you expect to find there?

14. What are the similarities and differences between cliffs and beaches?

⑮ Complete the sentences.

a. ... are the highest landforms.
b. ... are flat areas which are usually very fertile.
c. Rivers often run through ... , which are areas between mountains.
d. ... are flat or hilly areas, about 650 metres above sea level.
e. ... are very high flat areas.

⑯ Copy and complete these phrases in your notebook using the most appropriate terms.

“The lithosphere is a layer of the geosphere composed of ... materials, which are broken up into ... . These plates float on top of ... in the mantle. This causes the plates to ... . When two plates meet a ... occurs. When two plates move further apart ... occurs. Both events constitute ... formation.

The relief of the Earth's surface is formed by the interaction between ... forces and external ... .

This interaction gives rise to landforms, which are classified into three groups: ... , ... and ... .”

⑰ Copy and complete the world map below.

a. Identify the continents and oceans using the numbers that appear on the map.
b. Locate the islands that you have read about in this unit.

⑱ Look at the photos. Identify the landforms and explain how you were able to recognise them.

A

B

C

D

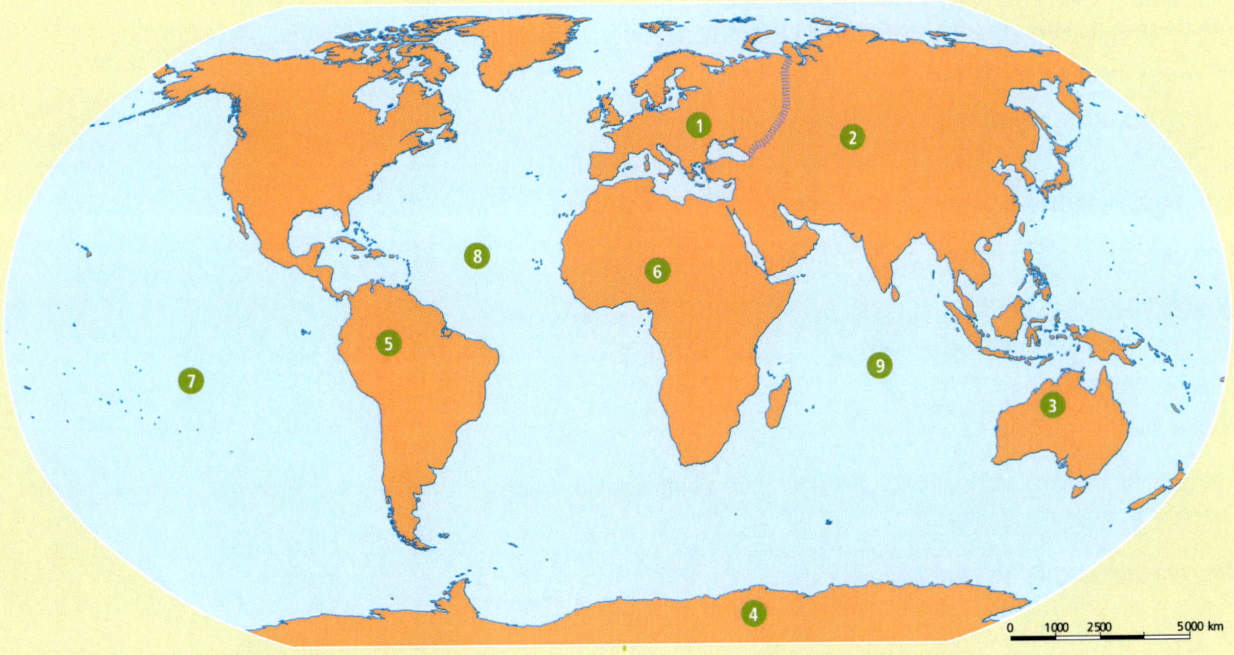

Read and think

SAND OR PEBBLES?

Some beaches are sandy, some are pebbly and some are even rocky. But why is this?

The shape of the coastline, the local geology and weather conditions are factors that determine what type a particular beach is. Another important factor is the sea and its waves. Remember that water is very good at erosion and it is constantly eroding the beach. The water washes land away, leaving debris behind. This debris becomes the beach. If the waves are very strong, the particles they leave are large and could be pebbles or even large rocks.

Powerful waves wash away all the small particles of sand. However, if the waves are small and gentle, they don't have the power to wash as much away, so they leave a soft sandy beach.

You may be on a sandy beach, but as you get near the sea, the beach feels different under your feet. The grains of sand become thicker. This is because the waves are stronger there and are washing away the finer sand, leaving the larger particles.

Sandy beaches are usually more popular. For this reason, people have created artificial beaches, where the sand is transported from other places. For example, Playa de los Amadores in Gran Canaria is a very beautiful beach, but it is not a natural beach, it is human-made!

Playa de los Amadores (Gran Canaria)

ANSWER THE QUESTIONS

1. Are these statements true or false? Correct the false ones in your notebook.
   a. Waves are not the only factor affecting beaches.
   b. Beaches are sandy when the waves are strong.
   c. The sand near the sea is finer than the rest of the sand on a beach.
   d. Artificial beaches are usually made of sand.
2. Find words in the text that mean the following:
   a. covered in small stones
   b. the remains of something broken
   c. very strong
   d. less fine
3. Can you think of any artificial landform other than a human-made beach? Describe its main characteristics.
4. Why are the beaches on coral islands sandy?
5. Why is the sand on some beaches in Tenerife (Islas Canarias) black?

Work it out

CONCEPT MAP

Use the words in the word cloud to create your own unit map in your notebook. Write any connecting texts you need.

continental points transportation peninsulas glacial plains
faults internal forces types of relief
wind archipelagos continental shelves fluvial
coastal volcanic
continental slopes valleys
The Earth's relief
ría deposition erosion ocean
ocean basins
plateaus bays biological
causes freezing and thawing mountains capes folding
gulfs
islands ocean ridges coastal external agents ocean trenches

SELF-ASSESSMENT

Carry out a self-assessment of what you have learnt in this unit. Choose one answer for each question and then check your answers.

1. The lithosphere is formed of:
   a. the mesosphere and the mantle.
   b. the crust and the upper part of the mantle.
   c. The upper part of the crust and the mantle.
2. When tectonic plates made of hard materials collide, the following type of mountain formation occurs:
   a. folding
   b. volcanic
   c. fault-block
3. Biological erosion is caused by:
   a. water and small creatures.
   b. plants and people.
   c. changes in temperature.
4. The lowest continental landforms are ...
   a. plateaus
   b. plains
   c. valleys
5. A small gulf is called ...
   a. an inlet
   b. a cape
   c. a bay
6. Altitude is ...
   a. the elevation of relief above sea level.
   b. the steepness of relief.
   c. the distance between the base and summit of a mountain.
7. Ocean ridges are found ...
   a. near the coast.
   b. next to continental shelves.
   c. in the middle of the ocean.
8. The largest continent is ...
   a. Asia
   b. Africa
   c. Europe
9. You can find more islands in ...
   a. Oceania and Asia combined.
   b. Europe.
   c. Africa and Europe combined.
10. Climographs, population pyramids and pie charts are ...
    a. maps
    b. graphs
    c. cartographic instruments

03 The Earth's surface

<< LOOKING BACK

- What is the external layer of the geosphere called?
- How are mountains formed?
- How do external agents affect relief?
- Approximately what percentage of the Earth is covered by water?
- How can we represent the Earth?

Colorado plateau, Arizona

Snaefellsnes peninsula, Iceland

active volcano

Guilin mountains, China

Islands, Palau

A mountain walk across Europe

In 1992 Nicholas Crane, a British geographer, explorer and writer, embarked on a new adventure: to walk across Europe along its mountain ranges. It took him about 18 months to travel alone from Cape Finisterre in Spain to Istanbul in Turkey. He met people of all types on his way but always refused one particular offer of help: traveling in a motorised vehicle. Early on in his journey, he abandoned his tent; he realised that it was more important to travel light, given the difficulty of some of the terrain he had to cross.

Crane told one interviewer that three things were essential for his expeditions: a compass, a map and an umbrella. He said, *I started using an umbrella when I was walking across Europe and noticed the Spanish shepherds carrying them. It looked a bit strange, but I found out that - apart from the obvious - they use them for shade during siesta. And they're also good for fighting off wild dogs. What's more, you can have the most expensive jacket in the world, but it doesn't keep your notebook dry when you're taking notes. An umbrella does.*

?

- Which mountain chains do you think he crossed to get from Cape Finisterre to the Pyrenees?
- Can you name any of the mountain ranges between the Pyrenees and Istanbul?

LOOKING FORWARD >>

- What landforms make up the territory of Spain?
- What are the largest peninsulas in Europe?
- Which African desert is the largest?
- Which mountain range is home to the tallest South American mountain?
- Where are the highest mountains in the world located?
- Is Australia an island or a continent?
- What are contour lines on topographic maps?

1 Land relief in Spain

What landforms make up the territory of Spain?

Spain is the fourth largest country in Europe with a surface area of 505 989 km^2. Its territory includes:

- Most of the Iberian Peninsula.
- The archipelagos of the Islas Baleares and the Islas Canarias.
- The cities of Ceuta and Melilla.
- Small archipelagos such as the Chafarinas Islands, the Columbretes Islands and Alborán Island.

Spain is the second highest country in Europe with an **average altitude** of 660 m above sea level.

DID YOU KNOW?

CEUTA AND MELILLA

The cities of Ceuta and Melilla are on the Mediterranean coast of North Africa.

Both cities have been part of Spanish territory since the 16th century.

1.1 The Meseta

The **Meseta Central** is the major landform on the peninsula. It is surrounded by mountain chains. The Meseta slopes towards the west which is why the rivers that cross the Meseta flow into the Atlantic Ocean.

The **Sistema Central** mountain chain runs across the Meseta from east to west. This chain includes the Gredos, Somosierra and Guadarrama mountain ranges. The Sistema Central divides the Meseta into two sections.

1 Submeseta Norte

The Submeseta Norte has an average altitude of 750 m and is occupied by the Duero watershed. It is characterised by flat landforms and highlands.

2 Submeseta Sur

The Submeseta Sur has an average altitude of 650 m. It is crossed by the Montes de Toledo, which separate the Tajo and Guadiana watersheds.

The middle part of the Submeseta Sur is called La Mancha.

1.2 The mountains bordering the Meseta

The Meseta is surrounded by different mountain chains. The major ones are:

Montes de León

The Montes de León connects the Submeseta Norte with the Macizo Galaico. It has peaks over 2 000 m, such as El Teleno (2 188 m).

Cordillera Cantábrica

The Cordillera Cantábrica runs parallel to the Costa Cantábrica. In its central section are the Picos de Europa, the area with the highest mountains, including Torre Cerredo (2 648 m) and Naranjo de Bulnes (2 519 m).

Sierra Morena

The Sierra Morena separates the Submeseta Sur from the Depresión del Guadalquivir. There are no mountains of significant height in this range.

Sistema Ibérico

The Sistema Ibérico separates the Meseta from the Depresión del Ebro. Its main mountain ranges are:

- To the west, the Sierra de la Demanda and the Picos de Urbión.
- In the centre, the Sierra del Moncayo. The highest mountain in this range is El Moncayo (2 313 m).
- To the east are the Serranía de Cuenca and the Albarracín and Gúdar mountain ranges.

1.3 Depressions

Depressions are vast flat areas, surrounded by mountain ranges and crossed by rivers. There are two depressions on the Iberian Peninsula:

Depresión del Ebro

The Ebro crosses a large, triangular **basin**. It is surrounded by the Pyrenees, the Sistema Ibérico and the Cordillera Costero-Catalana. The landforms are flat and stepped.

Depresión del Guadalquivir

The Guadalquivir runs through a large triangular valley which is open to the sea and surrounded by the Sierra Morena mountain range and the Sistemas Béticos. The landforms are low and flat.

1.4 Other mountain ranges

There are other mountain chains which do not border the Meseta.

Pyrenees

The Pyrenees is a major mountain range with the highest mountains on the Iberian Peninsula. It is made up of two groups of mountains:

- The **Axial Zone** is a group of high mountains. In the central area there are mountains of over 3 000 m; for example, the Aneto is 3 404 m.
- The **Pre-Pyrenees** is a group of low mountains located between the Depresión del Ebro and the Axial Zone.

The Axial Zone, Benasque (Huesca)

Sistemas Béticos

This group forms the longest group of mountains in Spain. It covers around 660 km from the Estrecho de Gibraltar to Cap de la Nao. It is made up of two mountain ranges:

- The **Sistema Subbético** runs from Cádiz to Alicante. It borders the Depresión del Guadalquivir. The range includes the Sierra de Cazorla, Sierra de Segura, Sierra de Aitana and Sierra de Mariola.
- The **Cordillera Penibética** runs parallel to the Mediterranean coast and includes the Sierra Nevada, where Mulhacén (3 481 m), the highest mountain on the Iberian Peninsula, is located.

Sierra Nevada, in the Cordillera Penibética

Macizo Galaico

It is made up of small mountains. The mountains are separated by sunken areas or **troughs**. The highest mountain is Cabeza de Manzaneda (1 778 m).

Montes Vascos

It is made up of low mountains separated by deep valleys. The highest mountains are Aitxuri (1 551 m) and Aitzkorri (1 544 m).

Cordillera Costero-Catalana

The Cordillera Costero-Catalana is a double mountain range parallel to the Mediterranean. It has no large mountains. The highest mountain is Turó de l'Home (1 712 m).

1.5 Island relief

Spain has two main groups of islands:

- The **Islas Baleares** are located in the Mediterranean Sea. The archipelago is made up of the islands of **Mallorca**, **Menorca**, **Ibiza**, **Formentera** and **Cabrera**.
- The relief of these islands, except for Menorca, is a continuation of the Sistemas Béticos. The highest mountains are in the Sierra de Tramontana range, in Mallorca.
- The **Islas Canarias** are located in the Atlantic Ocean. The archipelago is made up of the islands of **Lanzarote**, **Fuerteventura**, **Gran Canaria**, **Tenerife**, **Gomera**, **La Palma** and **El Hierro**.

  They are volcanic islands. Teide is a volcano located on Tenerife. At 3 718 m it is the highest mountain in Spain.

Sierra de Tramontana (Mallorca)

Teide (Tenerife)

1.6 The coasts of Spain

Spain has a very long coastline which is divided into five sections.

a The **Costa Cantábrica** has high, rocky relief. There are small inlets that form bays and rías.

b The **Costa Atlántica-Gallega** has mountainous relief and deep rías.

c The **Mediterranean coast** is the longest section of coastline. It is made up of beaches separated by rocky relief.

d **Island coasts**:

Along the coast of the Islas Baleares, rocky areas alternate with small beaches and coves.

The coasts of the Islas Canarias are mainly made up of rocky areas and cliffs.

There are many beaches on the eastern islands.

e The **Costa Atlántica-Andaluza** is made up of low areas with beaches, dunes and marshes.

ACTIVITIES

1. Make a map showing Spain's different types of relief with its main geographical features.
2. Make a list of the similarities and differences between the Pyrenees and the Sistemas Béticos. Do the same for the coasts of the Islas Baleares and the Islas Canarias.
3. What is the longest coastline in Spain?
4. Which landform is it?
   a. It occupies a large area of Spain and is surrounded by mountains.
   b. This mountain chain separates central Spain from the Depresión del Ebro.
   c. One side of this depression is surrounded by the sea.
   d. It is the highest mountain chain in Spain.
   e. El Hierro is one of the islands in this archipelago.

2 Land relief in Europe

Europe is on average the least mountainous continent. Its average height is only 340 m. The relief of Europe includes the following landforms:

COASTS

Europe has around 43 000 km of coastline. Its coasts are generally highly irregular in form.

Peninsulas include the Scandinavian Peninsula, Jutland, the Iberian Peninsula, Italy and the Balkan Peninsula.

Cliffs and fjords are common in areas where mountains meet the sea, for example, on the Atlantic coasts.

Cliffs in Normandy, France

Beaches are common in the south of Europe, especially along the coasts of the Mediterranean, Adriatic or Tyrrhenian. There are also many beaches on the Baltic coast.

ISLANDS

Europe's islands include very large islands, such as the British Isles in the Atlantic Ocean, and smaller islands in the Mediterranean Sea, such as the Islas Baleares.

Ibiza Es Vedra island in Mediterranean Sea

What are the largest peninsulas in Europe?

PLAINS

Plains occupy most of the surface of Europe. The Great European Plain extends across the middle and east of the continent.

Flowers field in Belarus

MASSIFS

Europe's massifs are old eroded mountains with **undulating** shapes. Examples include the Scandinavian Mountains, the Urals and the French Massif Central.

Ural Mountains

ALPINE MOUNTAIN RANGES

Alpine mountain ranges form a line of younger, higher mountains parallel to the Mediterranean Sea. They include the Pyrenees, the Alps, the Apennines, the Balkan Mountains and the Caucasus.

View of the Alps

ACTIVITIES

5. Which island or islands are these? Look at the map and decide.
   a. These islands are surrounded by the Atlantic Ocean and the North Sea.
   b. This island is in the Mediterranean Sea and has the Tyrrhenian Sea on one side and the Ionian Sea on the other.
   c. These Spanish islands are in the Mediterranean Sea.
   d. This island is surrounded by the Atlantic Ocean and the Irish Sea.
6. Find and write the names of the four highest mountains in Europe.

3 Land relief in Africa

Africa is the continent with the highest **average altitude**: 750 m. The main types of landforms are:

- **Plateaus** occupy almost 6% of the continent. Sometimes they are formed by deserts such as the Sahara, the world's largest desert, and the Kalahari.
- **Mountain ranges** include the Atlas Mountains in the north, and the Ethiopian Highlands, the Kilimanjaro Massif and the Drakensberg Mountains in the east.

The Sahara desert

Atlas Mountains

Drakensberg Mountains

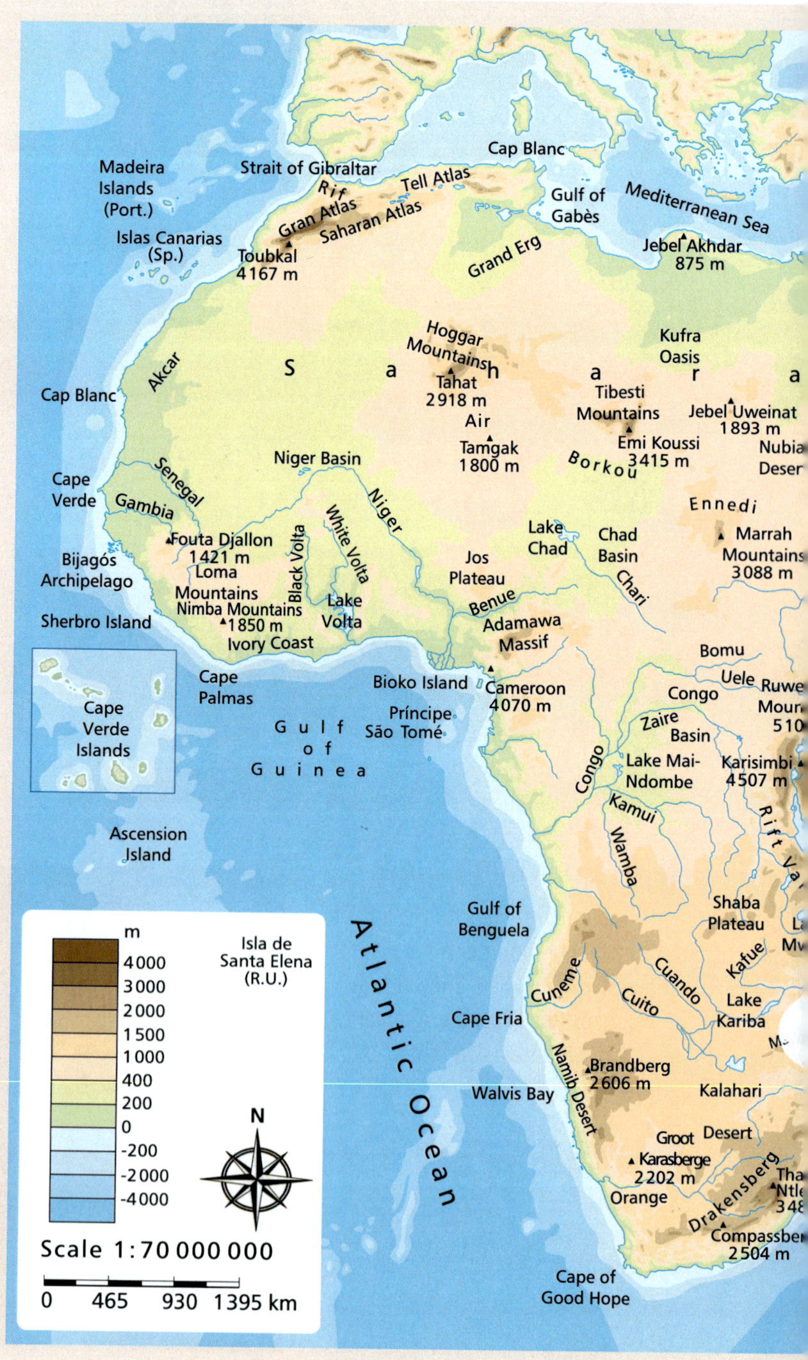

Which African desert is the largest?

Africa's mountains are mostly volcanic. Kilimanjaro (5 895 meters) is the highest mountain in Africa.

- **Coastal plains** are located between the plateaus and the coasts. They are long and narrow.
- **River valleys** such as those formed by the Nile and the Congo, or the valley occupied by Lake Chad.
- **Islands** are not a major feature, but important islands include Madagascar and the Islas Canarias and Seychelles archipelagos.

River Nile

Kilimanjaro

Seychelles

DID YOU KNOW?

THE RIFT VALLEY

The Rift Valley is an enormous tectonic fault of more than 4 800 km in length. It runs across the continent from the Red Sea to the Zambezi River valley. It is so large that it can be seen from space.

ACTIVITIES

7. Look at the map carefully. Are the following statements true or false?
   a. Africa's highest mountain is in East Africa.
   b. Lake Turkana is Africa's largest lake.
   c. The Kalahari Desert is the largest desert in Africa.
8. Look at the map of Africa and complete the table in your notebook.

Rivers	.....
Mountain ranges	.....
Highest mountains	.....
Deserts	.....

4 Land relief in America

The American continent contains two subcontinents: North and Central America, and South America. The main types of landforms are:

- **Mountain ranges** include the Appalachians and the Guiana Highlands in the eastern part of the continent. Mountain ranges like the Rocky Mountains, the Sierra Madre range and the Andes run along the Pacific coast. This area has the highest mountains on the continent.
- **Shields** are very large, low plateaus. Important examples are the Canadian Shield and the Brazilian Shield.
- **Plains** include the major continental plains crossed by large rivers, for example, the North American Great Plains and the vast Amazon Basin.
- **Islands and archipelagos** include the islands of the Caribbean and the islands of the Canadian coast, which include Greenland, one of the world's largest islands. Most of the important islands are located in the Atlantic Ocean.

The North American Great Plains

Which mountain range is home to the tallest South American mountain?

The Andes

Amazon Basin

ACTIVITIES

9. Where are the highest mountains in America?

10. Look at the maps and make a list of the similarities between North and South America.

11. Name three peninsulas in North America and four Caribbean islands.

5 Land relief in Asia

➲ Where are the highest mountains in the world located?

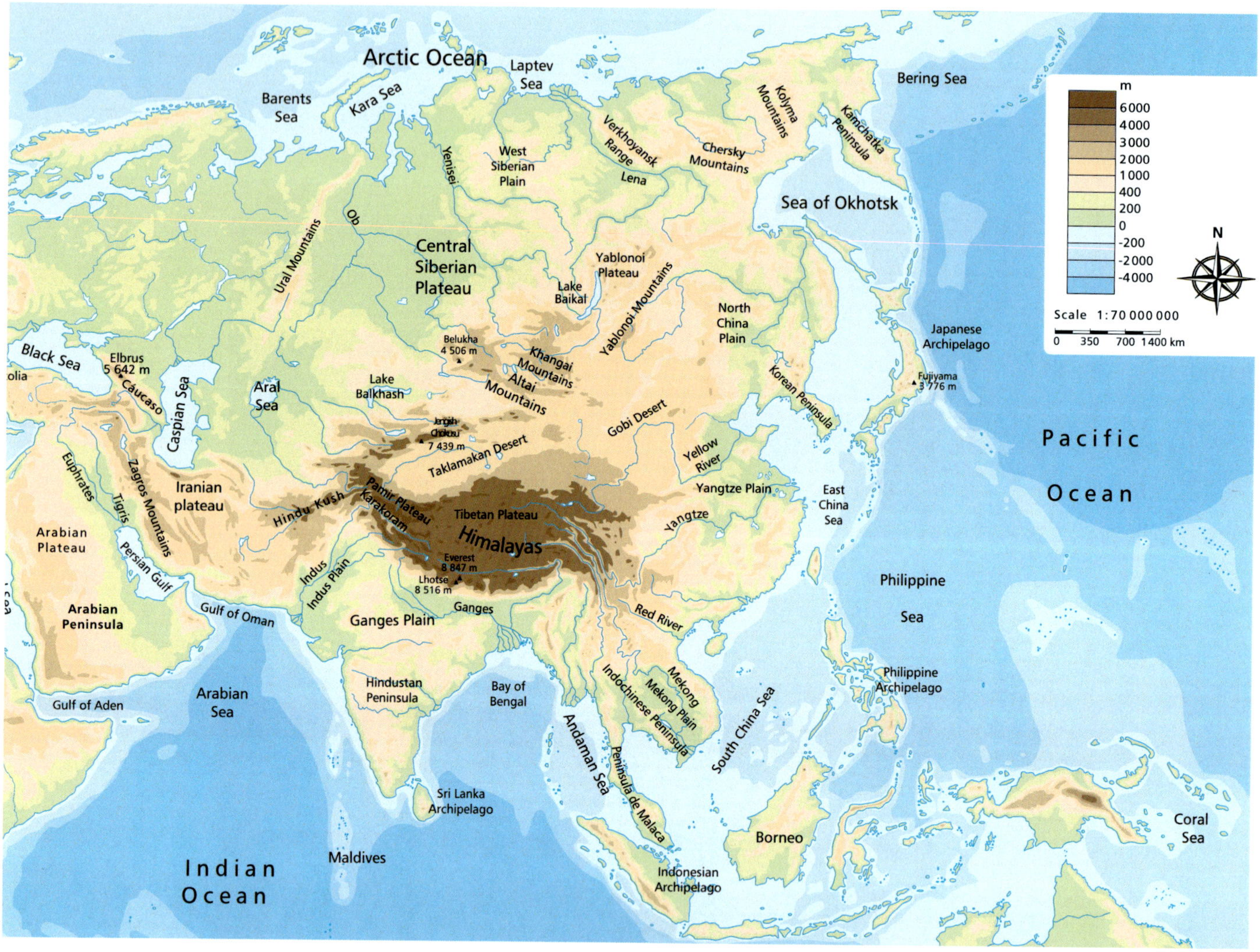

Asia is the largest continent in the world. It has a wide variety of landforms:

- **Plateaus** are found in the north and middle of the continent; for example the Central Siberian Plateau.

  The plateaus in the south, such as the Iranian plateau, are less extensive.

  The **high plateaus** of the Pamir Mountains and Tibet are also significant. The Tibetan Plateau is the world's highest and largest plateau.

- **Plains** cover most of Asia. Continental plains occupy part of Siberia. Alluvial plains are found around major rivers, such as the Yangtze, Indus, Mekong, Tigris and Euphrates.

- **Mountain ranges** include the great Himalayan mountain range, where the highest mountains on the planet are found. This is where Everest, the highest mountain in the world (8 848 m), is located.

ACTIVITIES

12. Look at the map and answer the questions.

a. What is the name of the highest plateau in Asia?

b. How high is Japan's highest mountain?

c. Where is Mount Elbrus?

d. At approximately what altitude is the Gobi desert?

13. Name three peninsulas and three archipelagos on the Asian continent.

6 Land relief in Oceania and Antarctica

Is Australia an island or a continent?

5.1 Land relief in Oceania

Oceania is the smallest continent. It is made up of different islands:

- **Australia** is the largest island in the world. Important features are the plateaus in the west, the plains of the central region and the mountains parallel to the east coast.
- **New Guinea**, **New Zealand** and **Tasmania** are medium-sized islands.
- **Melanesia**, **Polynesia** and **Micronesia** are archipelagos with two types of islands: volcanic islands and atolls.

Volcanic islands

They are characterised by a higher elevation in the centre and steep coasts.

Atolls

They are small and low coral islands, and may have a lake in the centre.

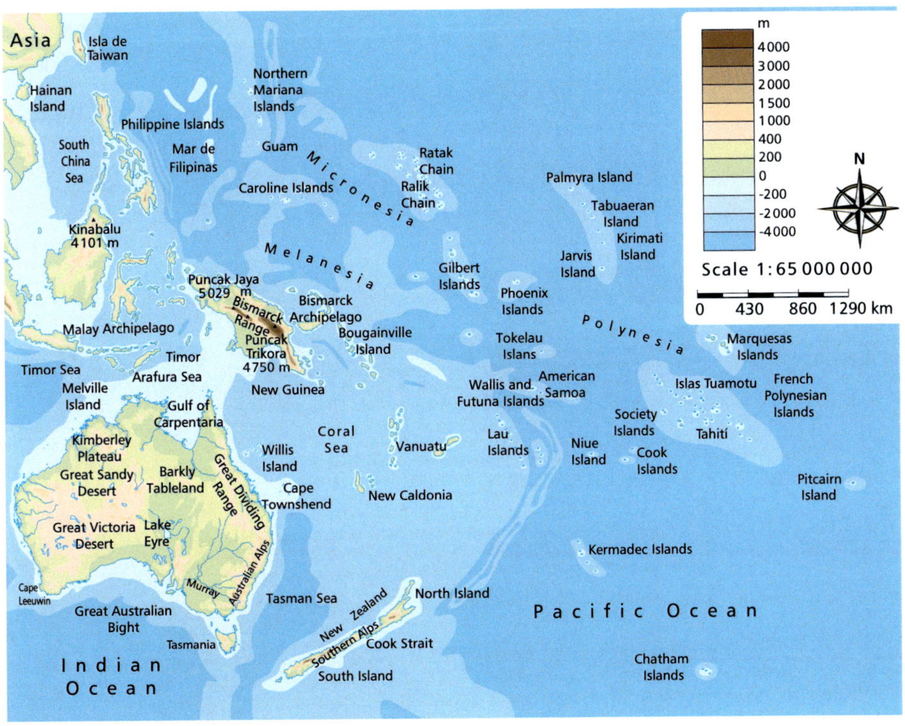

5.2 Land relief in Antarctica

The continent of Antarctica is located inside the Antarctic Circle. As a result, almost its entire surface is covered by ice.

Antarctica is made up of many islands and a large continental mass with the following important features:

- A large **plateau**.
- The **Transantarctic Mountains**, where the main mountains that emerge from the ice sheet are located, include Mount Vinson (5 140 m).

BIG THINKER

James Cook was a British navigator and explorer. He made three voyages across the Pacific Ocean.

He made maps of New Zealand and Australia. His description of the relief and islands of the Pacific helped improve the maps of the time.

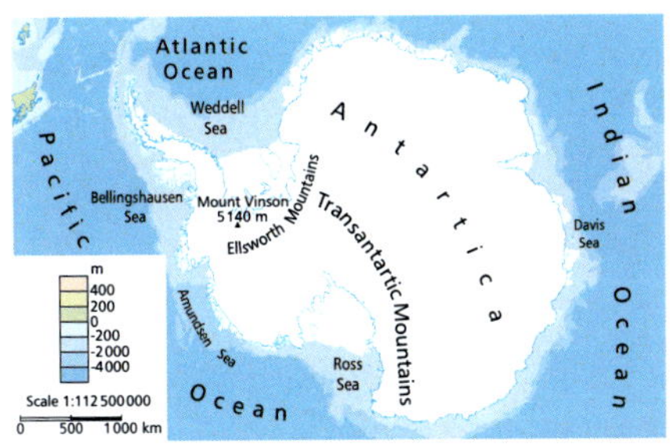

Map of Antarctica

ACTIVITIES

14. What two types of islands make up the archipelagos of Oceania?

15. In pairs, choose one of the archipelagos in Oceania. Using an encyclopaedia or the Internet, find out more about its relief. Present your findings to the class.

16. Answer the questions.

a. Why is Antarctica almost completely covered in ice?

b. What is the relief of Antarctica like?

Discovery techniques

HOW TO INTERPRET A TOPOGRAPHIC MAP

What is a topographic map?

A **topographic map** is a representation of the Earth's surface on a plane. A topographic map shows the following:

- Physical elements including, for example, relief, rivers and vegetation.
- Changes made by human beings such as centres of population and infrastructure.

Spain's National Geographic Institute produces the **National Topographic Map** of Spain which shows the entire territory of Spain. It is impossible to represent this entire area on a single plane. This is why the map is divided into 1 130 sheets. Each sheet represents a different area of the territory. The sheets are numbered and organised in consecutive order.

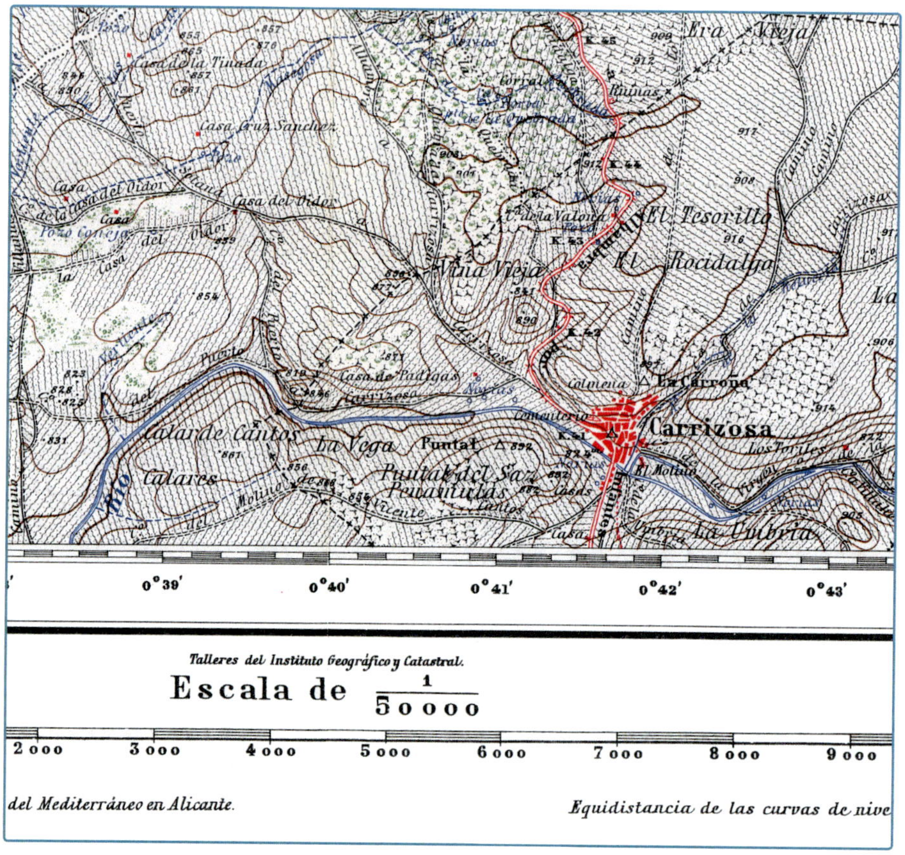

Orientation. Maps always have a northern orientation.

Location. Geographic coordinates, longitude and latitude, are shown in the margins.

- Triangulation station
- Provincial boundary
- Municipal boundary
- Arable land
- Arable land and scrubland
- Vineyard
- Olive grove
- Olive grove and vineyard
- Forest
- Scrubland
- Pasture
- Power line

What are contour lines on topographic maps?

How do you analyse and interpret a topographic map?

In order to analyse a topographic map correctly, you have to use the **key**. The key is a group of symbols that allow you to identify the natural and artificial features of the area mapped. The most important are:

1. The landforms or **altitude**.

   Because the real landforms are three-dimensional, they are represented on paper using contour lines and map colours:

   - **Contour lines** are imaginary lines which connect points of the same altitude.

     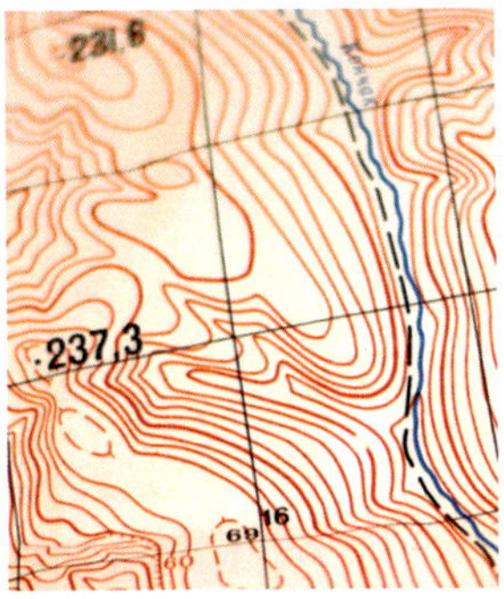

     Contour lines are brown for land areas (altimetry) and blue for ocean areas (**bathymetry**). They are drawn every 20 m. Every 100 m there are thicker lines called index contours.

     A map shows different types of areas. Many contour lines close together on a map show a steep slope; few lines far apart show a flat area.

   - **Map colours** are different colours which make it possible to represent areas of the same height. Green is usually used for low areas, ochre for intermediate areas, brown for high areas and white for altitudes above 3 000 m.

2. **Mountain peaks** are represented by a small triangle. Next to the triangle is the name of the mountain and its altitude.
3. **Hydrography:** All bodies of water (seas, lakes, rivers, streams and marshes) are shown in blue.
4. **Natural vegetation** and **crops** are shown using different green symbols. These symbols should be identified in the key.
5. **Centres of population** such as cities and towns are shown in red. The size of the dot indicates their importance.
6. **Communication routes:**
   - Roads are represented by solid red lines.
   - Trails and paths are represented by **dashed** black lines.
   - Railway lines are represented by black lines crossed by perpendicular segments.
7. **Place names** are the names of the features represented.
8. **Administrative boundaries** are the **boundaries** of municipalities, provinces, autonomous communities and countries. They are represented by different styles of dashed black lines.

PRACTISE WHAT YOU'VE LEARNT

1. Look at the topographic map on page 56 and answer the following questions.
   a. What are the significant landforms? Where are the biggest differences in elevation?
   b. What bodies of water are shown? Which are the largest?
   c. Are the population centres large or small? What are their names?
   d. Name the main examples of infrastructure shown on the map.
   e. Does the map show an urban or a rural area? Is it on flat or steep relief? Is there more natural vegetation or agricultural crops?
2. Go to the National Geographic Institute website (www.ign.es), where you can obtain important geographic information about Spain. Click on the *Cartoteca* (map library) section, where you can access the sheet with the map of your town. Once you have the map, write an analysis of it covering the following:
   a. Are there any major differences in elevation? What features on the map helped you see these?
   b. Are there any bodies of water? How big are they? Are they marine or continental?
   c. What infrastructure built by humans is shown on the map?
   d. Are there more natural areas or areas transformed by humans?

Revision activities

1. In pairs, write definitions for the following terms: *plains, gulf, continent, Himalayas, Pyrenees* and *the Islas Canarias.*

2. Copy and complete this chart with information on the Iberian Peninsula:

The relief of the Iberian Peninsula			
Meseta Central	Mountains bordering the Meseta	Other mountain ranges	Depressions

3. What is the highest peak in each mountain range in Spain? Make a list in order of height from the highest to the lowest.

4. Look at the map on page 44 and write the names of the mountains surrounding the Ebro and the Guadalquivir depressions.

5. How do landforms influence people's lives? Think of examples to help you answer this question.

6. What landforms can be found in your autonomous community? Give a detailed answer and explain how they affect life there.

7. In reference to the map on page 44, do you think travel and communication between different regions of the Iberian Peninsula was easy or difficult in the past? Explain your answer.

8. Work in pairs. Use the Internet if necessary. What part of Spain would you recommend to a foreign family who want to live in a place where ...
   a. they can go skiing for as many weeks a year as possible?
   b. they'll have fertile land to start a small fruit and vegetable farm?
   c. they'll be close to both the mountains and the sea?

   Present your answers to the class and justify them.

9. List the European peninsulas, starting from the north, and identify the seas, oceans or other bodies of water that surround each one.

10. Write the name of five European islands that are not Spanish.

11. Compare European massifs and alpine mountain ranges. What are the differences between them? List examples of both.

12. What are the five highest peaks in Europe? What mountain ranges do they belong to? Decide whether each of them are massifs or alpine mountain ranges and explain why.

13. What are the names of the seas and other bodies of water that surround Asia?

14. What is the mountain range in the north of Africa called? Investigate the origin of its name. Identify its highest peak.

15. Look for one African mountain range of higher altitude than the one in the previous activity and another one of lower altitude. Where are they located?

16. In which African mountain range are the highest peaks of the continent? Identify at least three mountains that are located there.

17. Copy and complete this chart in your notebook:

Land relief in America		
	NORTH AMERICA	SOUTH AMERICA
Mountain ranges		
Shields		
Plains		

18. Look for the highest mountain in North America. Identify the mountain range where it is located. Then, look for three South American mountains that are higher than this peak.

19. What is the highest peak in Asia? Look at the map on page 52 and identify the plateaus, plains and peninsulas surrounding it.

20. The highest peak in Oceania is Puncak Jaya. However, some geographers disagree with this and say that the highest peak is Mount Wilhelm. Use the Internet to find out and explain why this disagreement exists.

21. Investigate the meaning of the terms *ice sheet*, *sea ice* and *iceberg*. What relationship do they have with the Antarctica?

22 Match the correct altitude with each mountain:

• Puncak Jaya	• 6 961
• Mont Blanc	• 5 892
• Kilimanjaro	• 8 847
• Everest	• 4 884
• Mount Vinson	• 5 140
• Aconcagua	• 5 642

a. In which continents are they located?

b. Which mountain is the highest in the world? In which mountain range is it located?

c. Draw a bar graph that shows these mountains from highest to lowest. On the vertical axis, indicate the altitude in metres. On the horizontal axis, write the names of the mountains.

23 In which continent are the following landforms located?

The Gulf of Guinea, the Andes mountains, the Deccan Plateau, the Apennines, the Great Dividing Range, the Tibetan Plateau, the Drakensberg Mountains, the Caucasus, the Siberian Plateau, the Mount Vinson, the Ethiopian Highlands, the Himalayas, the Sierra Madre, the Ganges Plain, the Cape Horn, the Crimean Peninsula, the Korean Peninsula, the Rift Valley, the Kamchatka Peninsula, the Hudson Bay, the Persian Gulf, the Somali Peninsula, the Appalachians, the Cape of Good Hope, the Congo Basin, the Jura Mountains, the Rocky Mountains.

24 Investigate the meaning of the expression 'the Seven Summits'. What does this have to do with **mountaineering**?

25 What are some of the ways that people adapt to life in areas with steep mountains?

26 In groups, choose a continent to research. Create a map highlighting the most important features. Then, explain your findings to the class by creating a presentation on the continent's relief and its main characteristics, including its extent, main islands and coastal relief.

27 Play a game in small groups. Each group must write the name of a landform for each of the letters of the alphabet. You need to indicate the type of landform and the continent it belongs to. The group with the most names wins!

a. Example: A —> Aconcagua —> Mountain —> America

28 Guess the continent. Is it Asia, Africa, North America or South America?

a. The Andes are in this continent.

b. This continent has two very large deserts.

c. The longest river in the world is in this continent.

d. The Rocky Mountains are in this continent.

e. The highest mountain in the world is in this continent.

f. The Amazon River is in this continent.

g. Greenland is near this continent.

h. There are many islands in the east and southeast of this continent.

29 Complete the following table about land relief in Europe by looking at the map on pages 48-49.

Mountain range	Location
Caucasus	
Alps	
Pyrenees	Spain, ...
Urals	

30 Read the text and answer the questions.

> "On the one hand, and **chiefly** in groups of from eight to a dozen, volcanic islands rise above the sea; few reach an altitude of less than four thousand feet; their tops are often obscured in cloud. They are all covered in forests, all abound in food, and are all remarkable for **picturesque** and solemn scenery. On the other hand, we have annular islands, with a lagoon in the centre. They are rarely wider than half a kilometre and rarely reach the height of a man at their highest points."

Robert Louis STEVENSON. *In the South Seas.*

a. What types of islands does the writer refer to in the text?

b. What continent are they in?

c. What ocean are they in?

d. How are the two types of islands different?

Read and think

THE GOLD RUSH

1849. Somewhere on the East Coast of the United States at dinnertime...

– Did you hear about President Polk's speech, Jane?

– What about it, Adam?

– He said there really is gold in California. It isn't just a rumour. I think I should go. Finding gold will solve all our problems.

– But how can we pay for your journey? It's a long way and you'll need a lot of money to get there.

– Well, we have some savings. And if we need more money, I can borrow some. The only problem is you'll have to stay here and look after the children and the farm...

This conversation was probably similar to many conversations in the United States at the time.

A year earlier, James Marshall, a carpenter from New Jersey, had found gold in the American River at the foot of the Sierra Nevada Mountains in California. Not long afterwards, migrants arrived by boat from places like the Sandwich Islands (now Hawaii), Mexico, Chile, Peru and even China, in search of wealth.

By 1849, everybody in the United States had heard the news and many people spent everything they had to make the long journey to California. Thousands of potential gold miners, known as *'49ers*, travelled overland or by sea, sailing to Panama or even around Cape Horn in South America, to get to California.

To meet the needs of the *'49ers*, gold mining towns were created all over the region, with shops, saloons, and other businesses also trying to make their fortune from the Gold Rush. The towns were chaotic. There was little respect for the law. Robberies, gambling and violence were the order of the day. However, not everyone behaved **lawlessly** - some honest folk made a fortune from the Gold Rush too.

ANSWER THE QUESTIONS

1. Answer the questions.
   a. How did Adam think he could find the money for his journey?
   b. What did many women do when their husbands left for California?
   c. Where exactly was gold originally found?
   d. In your opinion, how did people from Hawaii, South America and China probably find out about the gold before people living on the East Coast of the United States?
   e. Who were the *'49ers*?
   f. In your opinion, how did the people who were not miners probably make their money?

2. Look at the map of North America on pages 52 and 53 and find Mount Whitney (in the Sierra Nevada). Then answer the questions.
   a. Approximately how far do you have to travel to get from Lake Michigan to Sierra Nevada?
   b. What type of territory do you have to cross? What obstacles are there?

3. Work in pairs to find out how the Gold Rush and Levi jeans are related. Present your findings to the class. Use pictures to show how jeans have changed since the 19th century.

Work it out

CONCEPT MAP

Use the words in the word cloud to create your own unit map in your notebook. Write any connecting texts you need.

America covered by ice continent massifs depressions largest Europe Asia archipelagos Spain meseta valleys plateaus landforms smallest **The Earth's surface** mountain ranges coasts plains highest Oceania subcontinents altitude Antarctica shields average islands Africa lowest

SELF-ASSESSMENT

Carry out a self-assessment of what you have learnt... in this unit. Choose one answer for each question and then check your answers.

1. Most of Asia is covered by ...
   a. mountains
   b. plateaus
   c. plains

2. The deserts in Africa are called ...
   a. the Sahara and the Gobi.
   b. the Kalahari and the Gobi.
   c. the Sahara and the Kalahari.

3. Madagascar is the name of ...
   a. a mountain.
   b. a desert.
   c. an island.

4. Both North America and South America have mountains ...
   a. in the north.
   b. in the west.
   c. in the east.

5. Australia is within the continent of ...
   a. Asia
   b. Oceania
   c. Antarctica

6. Mount Vinson is a high mountain in ...
   a. Asia
   b. Oceania
   c. Antarctica

7. Which of the following mountain ranges is in Europe?
   a. the Urals
   b. the Appalachians
   c. the Himalayas

8. Spain has a surface area of about ...
   a. 406 000 m^2.
   b. 506 000 m^2.
   c. 606 000 m^2.

9. The Submeseta Sur is separated from the Depresión del Guadalquivir by ...
   a. the Cordillera Cantábrica.
   b. the Sistema Subbético.
   c. the Sierra Morena.

10. The highest mountain range on the Iberian Peninsula is ...
    a. the Pyrenees.
    b. the Sistemas Béticos.
    c. the Montes de León.

11. On a topographic map, points of the same elevation are shown by ...
    a. curved lines.
    b. bent lines.
    c. contour lines

04 The hydrosphere

<< LOOKING BACK

- Where can we find water?
- What's the difference between an ocean and a sea?
- What is groundwater?
- What is a glacier? Where do glaciers form?
- What are the names of the oceans?
- Can you name a Spanish river?
- Where is the longest river in the world?

ocean water: an ocean swell

water in a solid state: an iceberg

Water, water everywhere...

According to the beliefs of Australian **aborigines**, there was a sacred era called 'The Dreaming' when spiritual beings created the world. During Dreamtime, an enormous frog drank all the water in the world and there was a drought: there was no water anywhere. The only way to finish the drought was to make the frog laugh. Animals came from all over Australia to try to make the frog laugh. In the end, the **eel** succeeded. The frog opened his eyes, his body quivered, his face relaxed and, at last, he laughed. His laugh sounded like thunder. The water poured from his mouth like a flood. It filled the rivers and covered the land.

- What happens if there is not enough water in a region?
- Where does the water in rivers and seas come from?

groundwater: source of the River Piedra

river water: waterfalls on the River Iguazú

LOOKING FORWARD >>

- What is the name given to water that has a moderate salt content?
- What is an aquifer?
- Which is the longest river on the Iberian Peninsula?
- Which rivers empty into the Black Sea?
- Where is the world's longest river?
- What is a river profile?

1 The hydrosphere

What is the name given to water that has a moderate salt content?

Three quarters of the surface of Earth's surface is covered by water.

- Water takes the form of solid, liquid or gas. Which form do you think is most common?
- The word **hydrosphere** refers to all the water on the planet, in all three states.

LIQUID

Most liquid water is **seawater** which is found in oceans and seas. A small percentage is **inland water**, which is made up of both **surface water** (lakes and rivers) and **groundwater** (underground water layers, known as **aquifers**).

Water exists in a liquid state **between 0 °C and 100 °C**.

All liquid water contains some salt, but it can be split into three different types, depending on the salt level:

- **Fresh water**: very low salt content (inland water)
- **Brackish water**: moderate salt content (inland water)
- **Salt water**: high salt content (seawater)

SOLID

Most solid state water exists as **snow and ice** in the polar ice caps and glaciers. Liquid water freezes **below 0 °C** and transforms into a solid.

Glaciers are large, semi-permanent bodies of solid water.

GAS

Water is considered a gas in the form of **water vapour**. Most water vapour exists in the Earth's atmosphere as evaporation from surface water. However, it can also come from inside the Earth in areas of **volcanic activity**.

Underground water vapour escapes from the Earth through volcanic geysers.

ORIGINS AND EVOLUTION

Our planet's water began as **water vapour** that existed 4.6 billion years ago. At this time the planet was a hot sphere formed of different materials. As **the planet cooled**, the atmospheric vapour condensed. This process formed clouds, followed by rain that produced seas over millions of years. The result of this long process was the formation of our **hydrosphere**.

THE COMPOSITION OF THE HYDROSPHERE

The hydrosphere has the following composition:

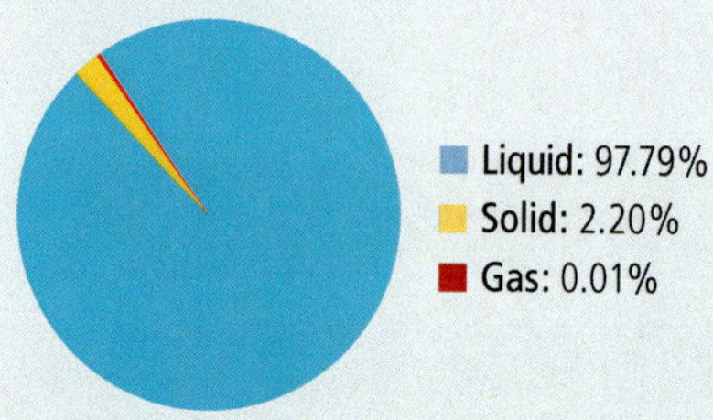

ACTIVITIES

1. What temperature does water have to be to exist in a liquid state?
2. What are the three types of liquid water and what makes them different?
3. How did the cooling of the Earth affect the water on our planet?

2 The distribution of water on Earth

What is an aquifer?

2.1 Water in seas and oceans

- Oceans are large bodies of water that **surround continents.**
- Seas are smaller. They are **partly surrounded by land** and form parts of oceans.

COMPOSITION

- Sea water is a **mixture of mineral salts**; the most common component is sodium chloride (common salt). It also contains a large quantity of magnesium salts.
- The **salt in seawater affects density**; water with a higher salt content has a greater density.
- Seawater temperature depends on latitude and depth. Areas that are more exposed to sunlight (lower latitudes) are warmer. Temperatures are lower in deeper bodies of water and warmer in shallower areas.

Most liquid water is seawater.

DID YOU KNOW?

Average waves are about three metres high. However, the tallest wave was over 30 metres high; nearly the height of a ten-storey building! It was recorded in Alaska in 1958.

What do you think caused it?

MOVEMENT

Oceans and seas move and change all the time in a variety of ways:

- **Waves** occur on the surface of the water. They are mainly **caused by the wind** and can vary in strength.
- Tides are the regular movements of the seas in which the sea levels rise and fall. This is caused by the gravitational force of the Sun and the Moon.
- **Ocean currents** are horizontal movements of water within seas and oceans. Currents have **distinct densities** and **temperatures**. They are important because they redistribute heat and salt to different areas of the Earth.

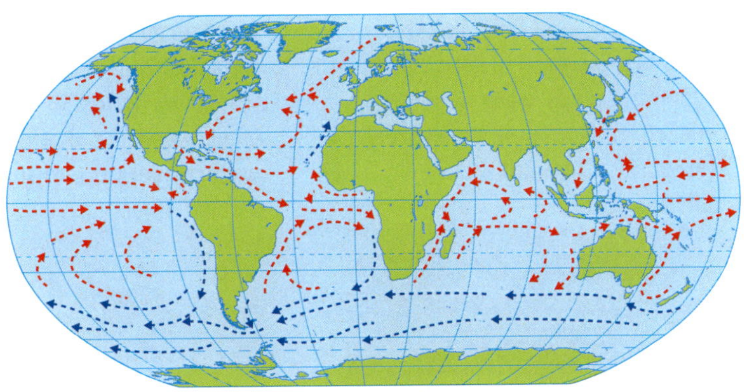

Warm currents
Cold currents

Map of the world's ocean currents

ACTIVITIES

4. What factors dictate the density and temperature of seawater?
5. What are the three ways in which water moves and what causes each of these movements?
6. Do you know what tsunamis are? Do tsunamis occur in the Mediterranean Sea? Investigate, and then write a report on your findings.

2.2 Inland water

Inland water includes **surface water** and **groundwater**, as well as **glaciers**.

SURFACE WATER

Surface water can be found on Earth in a variety of forms:

A river is a flowing body of fresh water. The route of a river is called its course. **The upper course** includes the source, where the river starts. The water moves very fast and has a powerful **erosive** force. Rivers form V-shaped valleys.

The **middle course** is longer and less steep. The water loses speed and the river begins to deposit the eroded sediment from the upper course. There are curves and bends called meanders.

A river from source to mouth

The **lower course** includes the final stretches of the river and the mouth. The river has a larger flow and deposits all the sediment it is carrying.

In rivers that flow into the sea, a wide **estuary** of brackish water can form from sea currents that transport river sediment. Estuaries and nearby coastal areas are often heavily **populated by humans**.

A **lake** is a body of fresh, brackish or salt water. The water in lakes comes from rivers, groundwater or from melted glaciers. Lakes are **entirely surrounded by land** and are different sizes.

Water accumulates from rain and groundwater in low-lying areas to form **wetlands**. Wetlands are often seasonal: **a shallow layer of water covers the ground** for only part of the year.

A **lagoon** is a shallow lake that **forms on coastlines**. Lagoons have at least one inlet from the sea.

ACTIVITIES

7. Why are V-shaped valleys formed in the upper course?
8. Which of the three courses of a river is best for agriculture? Discuss with a partner.
9. Describe the main difference between a lake and a lagoon.

GROUNDWATER

Groundwater is water that is stored underground, beneath the surface of the Earth.

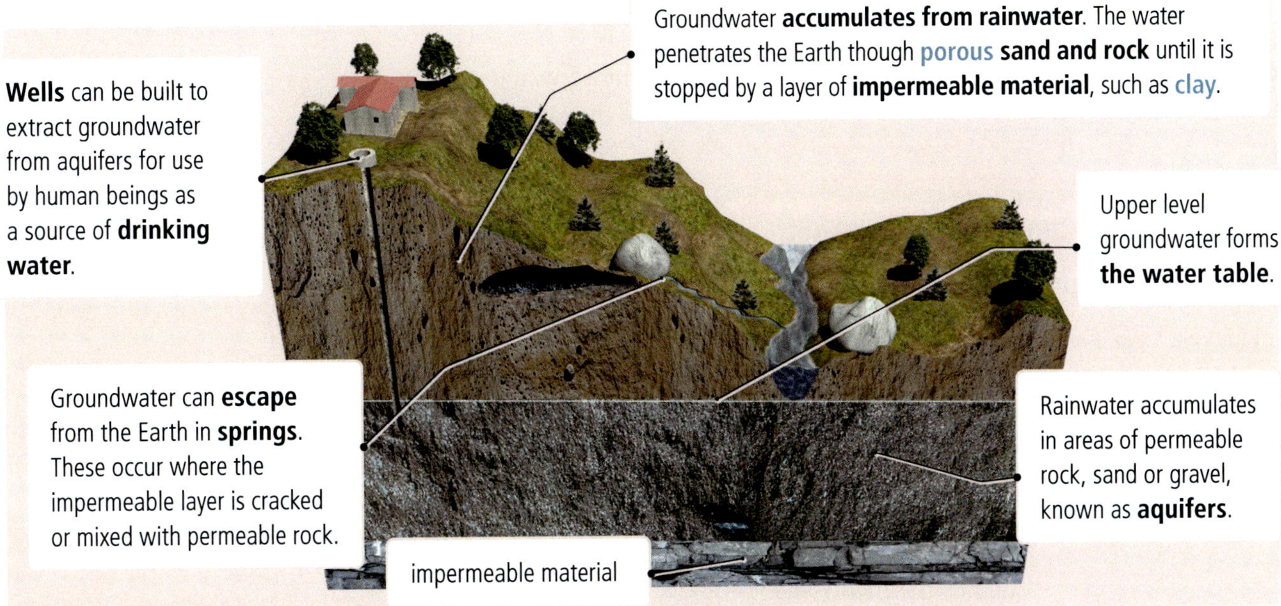

GLACIERS

Glaciers are large masses of **slow-moving ice**.

Glaciers can only exist in areas of the Earth where the temperature is always, or nearly always, **below 0 °C**.

U-shaped valleys were formed by glaciers in parts of the Earth that were once covered in ice.

Glaciers move downhill very slowly. This is because of their immense weight and the Earth's gravity. Their movement **erodes** the original landscape and forms **U-shaped valleys**.

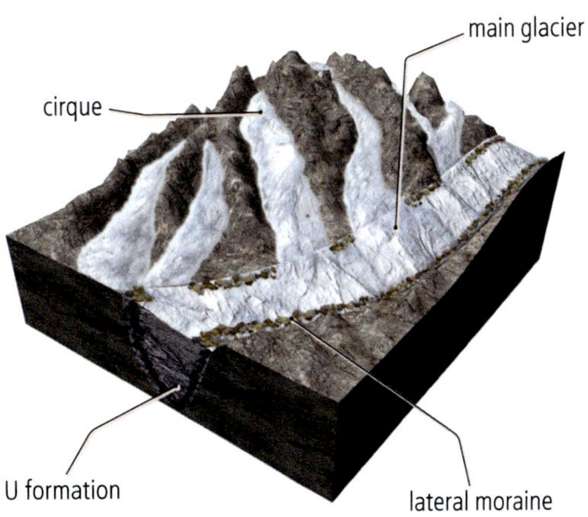

As they move, glaciers transport **moraines**. This rocky debris can be seen in sheets and piles where the glacier has passed or on the surface of the ice.

Icebergs are floating pieces of glacier that have reached the sea and broken off.

ACTIVITIES

10. Do glaciers tend to exist in lower or higher altitudes? And what type of latitude must they have in order to exist?

11. Have you ever heard the expression 'tip of the iceberg'? What does it mean?

12. On the previous page, you learned that V-shaped valleys form in the upper course of a river. Compare them with valleys formed by glaciers. Why do you think these are U-shaped?

3 The distribution of water in Spain

Which is the longest river on the Iberian Peninsula?

Water is not evenly distributed in Spain. Some areas have more water than others depending on factors such as geography or the amount of rainfall they receive.

3.1 Rivers of the Cantabrian watershed

- The rivers in this region are short, and empty into the Cantabrian Sea.
- They have a large flow because the area receives a lot of precipitation.
- These rivers have a steep gradient because the Cordillera Cantábrica is close to the sea.

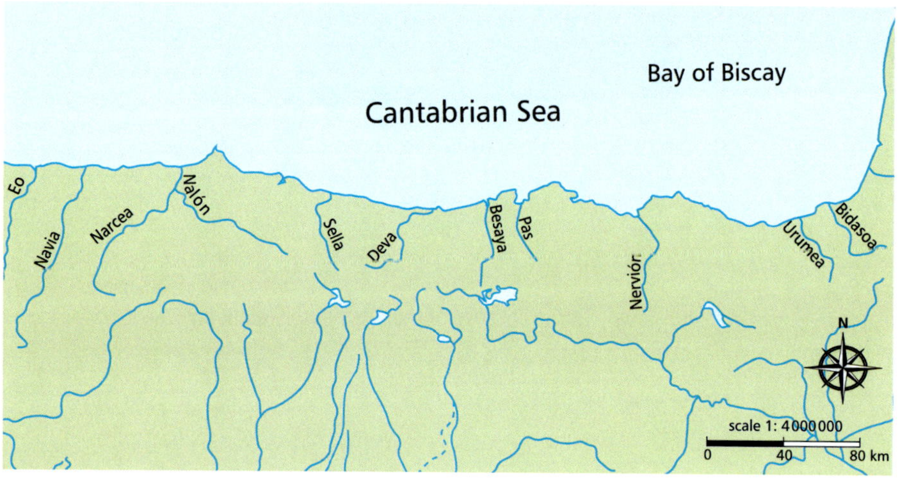

The erosive force of the Cantabrian rivers creates gorges and ravines. Estuaries and *rías* form at the river's mouth.

3.2 Rivers of the Atlantic watershed

Most of the rivers on the Peninsula empty into the Atlantic Ocean. The reason for this is that the Meseta is very large and slopes to the west.

The rivers of the Atlantic watershed can be divided into three groups.

GALICIAN RIVERS

Galician rivers have a very high flow due to the amount of precipitation in the area.

The most important Galician rivers are the Miño and its **tributary**: the Sil. Other important rivers are the Tambre and the Ulla.

The main characteristics of Galician rivers are the large *rías* that form at their mouths.

ACTIVITIES

13. List the main characteristics of Cantabrian rivers. Give at least three.

14. Read the description of Cantabrian and Atlantic rivers again and explain the influence relief has in the course and longitude of rivers.

15. What do Galician and Cantabrian rivers have in common? What is this due to?

RIVERS OF ANDALUCÍA

The rivers of Andalucía include the Guadalquivir, the Tinto, the Odiel and the Guadalete.

The Guadalquivir is one of the largest rivers in Andalucía. It begins in the Sistemas Béticos and empties into the sea at Sanlúcar de Barrameda.

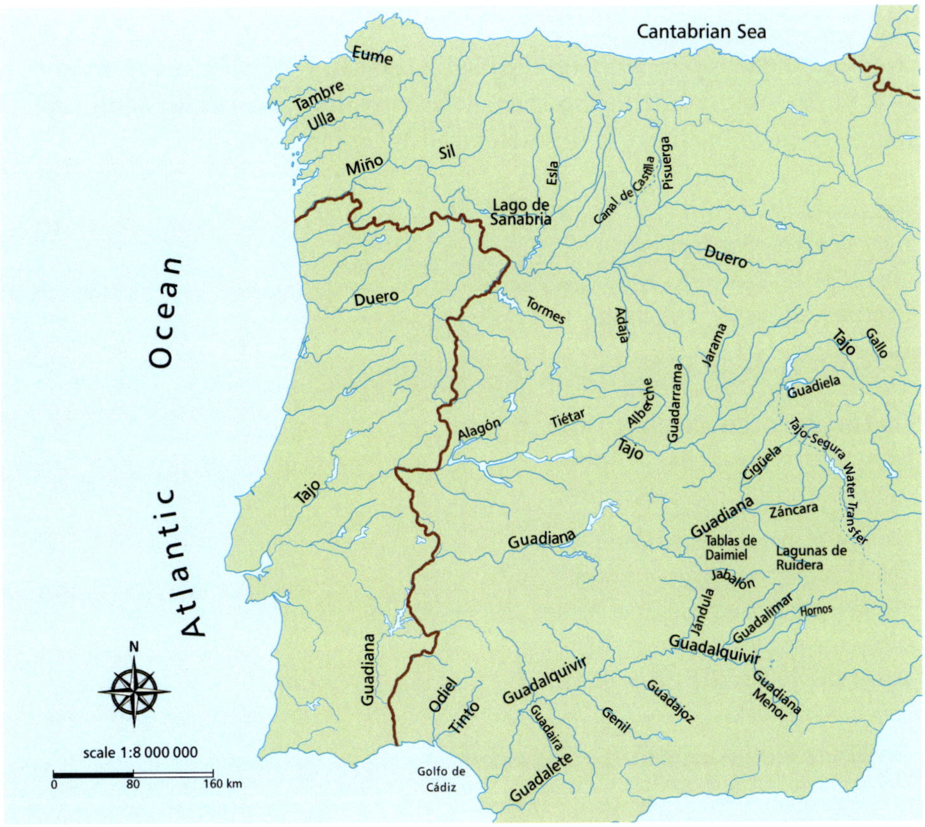

RIVERS THAT CROSS THE MESETA

The rivers that cross the Meseta have large river basins and very long courses. Important examples include:

The **Duero** is one of the rivers with the largest river basin and highest flow on the Iberian Peninsula. It begins in the Picos de Urbión, in the Sistema Ibérico, and runs across the Submeseta Norte. Its mouth is in Porto, Portugal.

The **Tajo** is the longest river on the Peninsula. It begins in the Sistema Ibérico and its mouth is in Lisbon, Portugal. The Tajo crosses the Submeseta Sur, forming a narrow river basin between the Sistema Central and the Montes de Toledo.

The **Guadiana** begins in the Lagunas de Ruidera and crosses La Mancha between the Montes de Toledo and the Sierra Morena. It empties into the sea at Ayamonte, Huelva.

ACTIVITIES

16. Make a list of the main rivers in Andalucía and the Meseta. Include their sources and their mouths.

17. Copy the map and colour each river and its main **tributaries** in a different colour in, e.g. Duero and its tributaries in red, Tajo and its tributaries in blue ... (draw only the rivers whose names appear on the map). Then, write their names.

18. Compare and contrast the rivers in Galicia with those that cross the Meseta.

3.3 Rivers of the Mediterranean watershed

Except for the Ebro, the rivers of the Mediterranean watershed are short and have a low flow. In different seasons of the year they experience significant changes in flow. The rivers in this watershed are grouped into:

Catalan rivers are short and have a continuous flow due to melting snowfall. Most of these rivers begin in the Pyrenees. Examples include the Ter and the Llobregat.

The **Levante rivers** are longer and begin in the Sistema Ibérico and the Sistemas Béticos, and cross broad coastal plains.

The flow of these rivers decreases significantly in the summer. However, between late summer and autumn, they experience a significant rise in water level due to the phenomenon known as the *gota fría* which causes **torrential** rain. Examples of Levante rivers are the Turia, the Júcar and the Segura.

Andalusian rivers are short and steep. They begin in the Sistemas Béticos.

In the summer they experience major changes in flow. During periods of torrential rains, the water level can rise significantly.

Examples of Andalusian rivers are the Guadalhorce and the Andarax.

The **Ebro** is one of the longest rivers on the Peninsula, with a length of 910 km. It has the largest river basin and the highest flow in Spain.

ACTIVITIES

19. Do you know what the *gota fría* is? Do some research and find out where, when and why it happens.

20. What is the most important difference between Catalan rivers and any other two groups of rivers on the Mediterranean watershed?

3.4 Island torrents

There are no major rivers on the Islas Baleares or the Islas Canarias due to their climate and relief.

However, these archipelagos have dry river beds that channel water during rainy periods. These river beds are called *torrents* on the Islas Baleares and *barrancos* on the Islas Canarias.

3.5 Aquifers, lakes, pools and wetlands

Aquifers are underground lakes. More than thirteen million people in Spain use water from aquifers for domestic purposes and irrigation. In the province of Almería, for example, 82% of drinking water comes from aquifers.

Wetlands are areas saturated with water, either permanently or seasonally. There are more than 150 000 wetlands in Spain.

There are no large lakes on the Iberian Peninsula due to its high altitude and the gradient of the relief. However, there are pools, above all on the Meseta and in mountain ranges.

Here are some of the main lakes, pools and wetlands in Spain:

BIG THINKER

Ramón Margalef was one of the most distinguished Spanish scientists of the twentieth century. He is considered one of the fathers of modern ecology. Initially, he dedicated his time to researching marine environments, but over time found that he preferred working with fresh water. In 1973, Margalef lead a programme that studied over one hundred lakes and reservoirs across Spain.

The **Lago de Sanabria** is the largest lake in Spain. It is a glacial lake located in the Montes de León. This type of lake is common in the highest mountain ranges.

The **Tablas de Daimiel**, in Castilla-La Mancha, are pools that are considered wetlands. Water accumulates in these areas because it does not have a natural outlet.

The **Lagunas de Ruidera** are a group of small lakes in Castilla-La Mancha. They are connected by underground channels and by small **waterfalls**.

The **Laguna de Gallocanta** is a very large pool in Aragón. It is linked to an important aquifer system and another smaller pool called Laguna de Zaida.

Albufera de Valencia is a wetland formed by a fresh water **lagoon** separated from the sea by a **sandbank**. Lagoons are common along the Mediterranean coast. Other examples include Albufera de Mallorca and the salt lakes of Torrevieja.

ACTIVITIES

21. Explain in your own words why there are no large lakes in Spain.

22. Take a blank physical map of Spain and locate these five main lakes, pools and wetlands mentioned on this page. Then, do some research about them and find out what kind of flora and fauna they have. What activities could you do there if you were to visit them? Which one would you prefer to go to?

4 The distribution of water in Europe

Europe has many rivers and lakes. Rivers are distributed in four major **watersheds**.

Arctic Ocean watershed

- The rivers of northern Europe empty into the Arctic Ocean.
- These rivers have a high flow. They freeze in winter.
- The most important ones are the Pechora and the Northern Dvina.

Atlantic Ocean watershed

- These rivers have a high flow due to the regular rainfall. The most important rivers are the Elbe, the Rhine and the Seine. Other rivers in this group, such as the Oder and the Vistula, empty into the Baltic Sea.
- Most of the Rhine, from the city of Basel to its mouth, is navigable. It is therefore one of Europe's most important transport routes.

Mediterranean Sea watershed

- These rivers are short and have an irregular flow due to summer **droughts**.
- Major rivers include the Rhône and the Po.

ACTIVITIES

23. What is the main difference between the rivers in the Arctic and the Atlantic watershed? What about the difference between the Atlantic and the Mediterranean one?

24. Compare a political map of Europe with the map above and write the names of the rivers that passes through each city: Paris, Zaragoza, Hamburg, Cologne, Kiev, Volgograd, Geneva, Warsaw, Vienna, Turin.

Which rivers empty into the Black Sea?

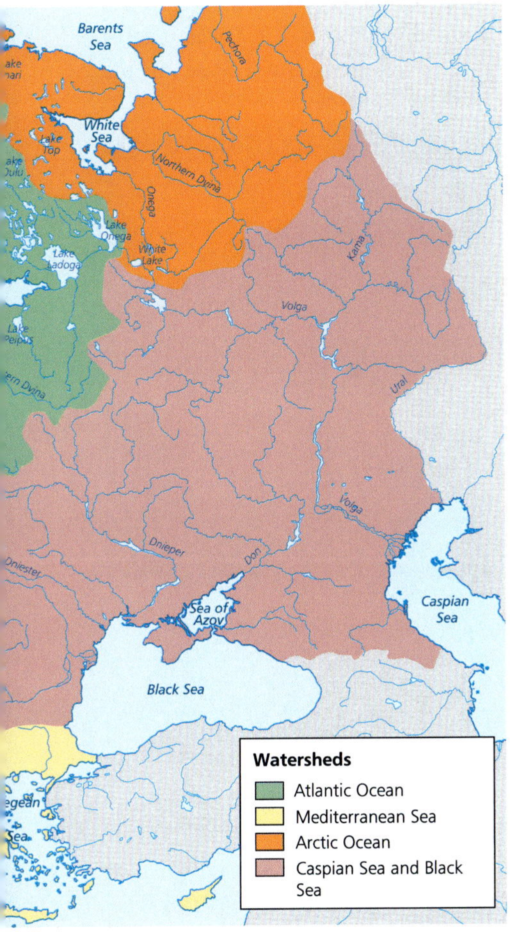

Black Sea coastline

Black Sea and Caspian Sea watershed

- These rivers are the longest on the continent. They run through the plains of Central Europe.
- Two of Europe's most important rivers empty into the Caspian Sea: the Volga, Europe's longest river, and the Ural, which forms the border between Europe and Asia.
- Other important European rivers empty into the Black Sea: the Danube, the Dniester, the Dnieper and the Don.

LAKES OF EUROPE

There are numerous lakes in Europe, but they are small.

Lakes of **glacial origin** are found in northern Europe, in Russia and Finland. The two largest lakes are located in Russia: Lake Ladoga and Lake Onega.

Alpine lakes, such as Lake Geneva and Lake Constance in the Alps, are smaller but very beautiful.

ACTIVITIES

25. Locate the Sea of Marmara which divides Turkey between Europe and Asia. Which two seas does it connect?

26. What makes the Caspian Sea different to other seas?

27. Which watershed do each of the following rivers belong to? Elbe, Po, Ural, Dniester, Vistula, Pechora.

5 The distribution of water in the rest of the world

Where is the world's longest river?

ASIA

Asia has both inland seas and lakes. Examples include the Caspian Sea, the largest inland sea in the world, and Lake Baikal, the deepest fresh water lake on Earth. Asia has long rivers with high flows. These rivers begin in inland mountain ranges and run across extensive plains.

The rivers of the **Arctic Ocean watershed** are long and freeze for several months during the winter.

The rivers of the **Indian Ocean watershed** have a high flow. This is because the distance from where they begin in the mountains to where they empty into the ocean is relatively short.

The rivers of the **Mediterranean watershed** are very short and do not have a very high flow.

The rivers of the **Pacific Ocean watershed** are long and run through extensive **alluvial** plains. One example is the Yangtze (Blue River): the longest river in Asia.

AFRICA

The distribution of rivers in Africa is influenced by the huge areas covered by deserts where there are very few rivers.

The rivers of the **Indian Ocean watershed** are shorter and also have a high flow.

The rivers of the **Atlantic Ocean watershed** are long and have a high flow.

The rivers of the **Mediterranean watershed** are short, with the exception of the Nile, which is the longest river in the world.

OCEANIA

Oceania is made up of groups of islands. They have few rivers and lakes. However, there are large rivers in Central Australia, such as the Murray.

DID YOU KNOW?

The Huang He or Yellow River is the second longest river in China. It takes its name from the colour of the sediment it carries.

ACTIVITIES

28. In what direction does the Nile flow?

29. Rivers in Southeast Asia suffer from periodic **flooding**. What could be the cause? What effects can this have on humans?

30. Look at the map on the next page and name two large African rivers that end in the Indian Ocean and two that end in the Atlantic.

THE AMERICAS

There are a lot of lakes in North America such as the Great Lakes: Superior, Huron, Michigan, Erie and Ontario. They form the largest group of lakes on Earth and contain a fifth of the fresh water on the Earth's surface. A very large South American lake is **Lake Titicaca**, which is between the Peruvian Andes and the Bolivian Andes. At an altitude of 3 815 m, Lake Titicaca is the highest **navigable** lake in the world.

In the Americas, the length and form of its rivers is influenced by their location in relation to the continent's eastern mountain ranges.

The rivers of the **Pacific Ocean watershed** are short because they begin near the coast.

The rivers of the **Arctic Ocean watershed** are not usually very long and remain frozen most of the year.

The rivers of the **Atlantic Ocean watershed** are long and have a high flow. They begin in the eastern mountains. The Amazon has the largest flow in the world.

ACTIVITIES

31. What is the main difference between rivers that end in the Pacific Ocean and rivers that end in the Atlantic ocean?

32. According to the map above, which continent has more rivers?

33. Along which main parallels, both sides of the Equator, are there less rivers? Why do you think this happens?

Discovery techniques

RIVER PROFILES

How to represent a river profile

A river profile is the visual representation of a river's course from its source to its mouth. It is represented using a **line chart**. The line chart is based on two axes of coordinates:

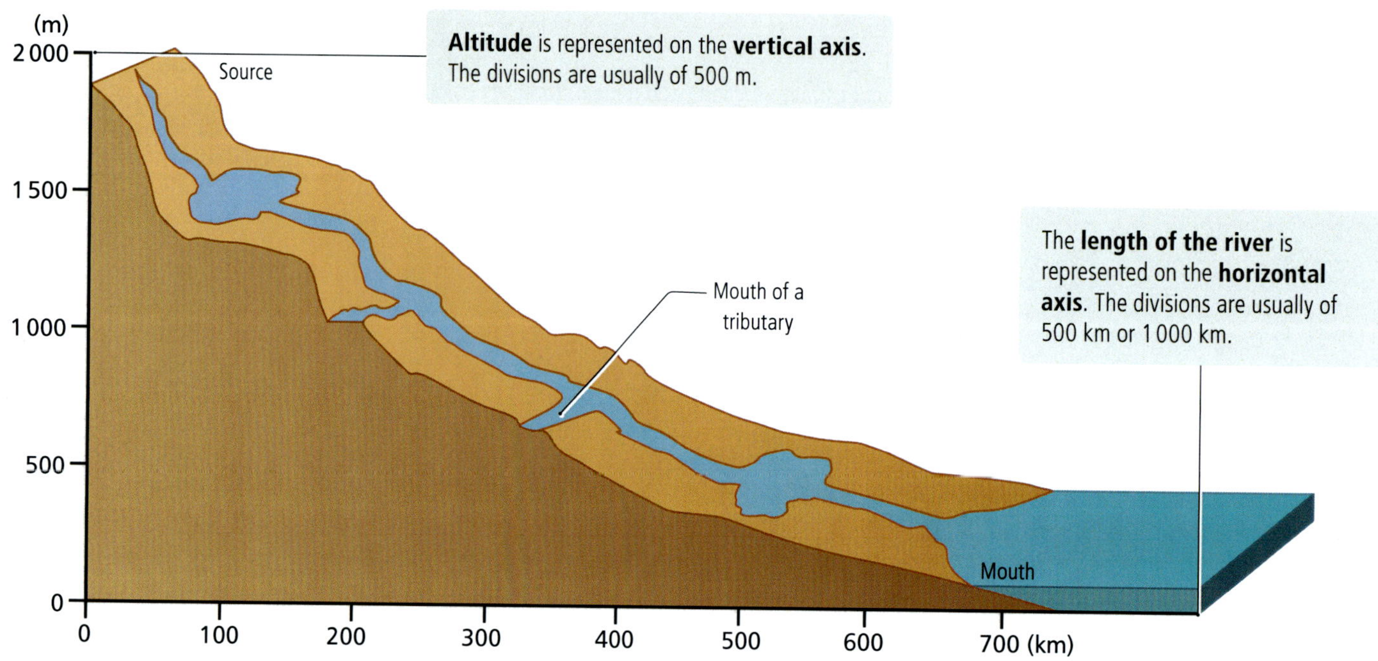

How to make a river profile

In order to make a river profile, you'll first need all the necessary data in table form. In this case, you are going to create a profile of the Tajo with the information in the table below. In it, you can identify:

The **altitude** of the river **source**.

A list of the **tributaries** that flow into the river.

The **distance** between one point on the river course and another, and the **total length** of the river.

Points along the river course	Altitude (m)	Length (km)
Source of the River Tajo	1 590	0
Mouth of the River Gallo	900	97
Mouth of the River Guadiela	820	240
Mouth of the River Jarama	480	374
Mouth of the River Guadarrama	420	450
Mouth of the River Alberche	360	547
Mouth of the River Tiétar	190	696
Mouth of the River Alagón	110	770
Mouth at the Atlantic Ocean	0	1 050

What is a river profile?

1. Look at and analyse the data for the coordinates (see table). Next, decide the **intervals** for the **coordinates** and indicate these on a piece of graph paper.
2. Next, represent the data:
   - The **source** is placed exactly on the vertical axis (altitude).
   - Places where a **tributary** enters the river are marked with a dot. The position of these dots is determined by their distance from the source of the river (horizontal axis) and their altitude (vertical axis).
   - The **mouth** of the river (where the altitude is 0 m) is placed exactly on the horizontal axis.
3. Connect all the points with a line. The line shows the profile of the river with differences in altitude.

River Tajo profile

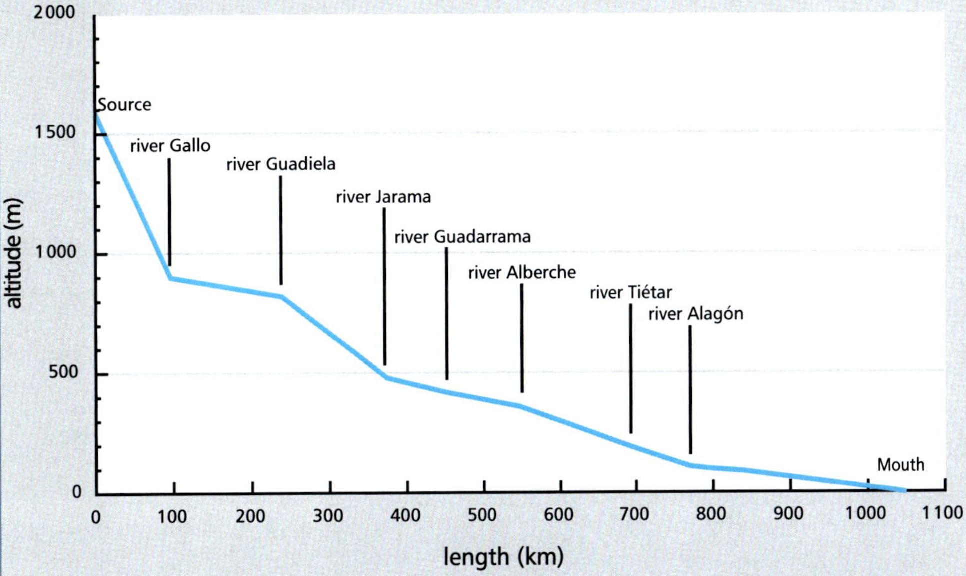

PRACTISE WHAT YOU'VE LEARNT

1. Draw a river profile for the Guadalquivir using the data in the table below.

Points along the river course	Altitude (m)	Length (km)
Mouth	1350	0
Mouth of the River Hornos	1090	55
Mouth of the River Guadiana Menor	900	145
Mouth of the River Guadalimar	800	200
Mouth of the River Jándula	300	285
Mouth of the River Guadajoz	200	444
Mouth of the River Genil	150	510
Mouth of the River Guadaira	50	600
Mouth at the Atlantic Ocean	0	657

Revision activities

1. Look at the map on page 75 and decide which hemisphere has more water.

2. Why do you think some rivers are larger than others? Make a list of the possible causes and share it with your partner.

3. On a blank sheet of paper, draw an imaginary landscape and label the water forms. Include, at least, all the following: *river, confluence, tributary, source, high course, waterfalls, middle course, meanders, low course, delta, mouth, sea, lake, lagoon, wetland, glacier.*

4. Through the process of **erosion**, the Colorado River dug out the Grand Canyon, which is 446 kilometers long and more than 1 600 meters deep. In some places, the canyon is greater than 25 km wide. How do you think erosion affects people living near a river?

5. Look at these pictures. They represent the three different courses of a river. Identify which course corresponds to each of them and name the geographical feature you can see in the pictures.

A

B

C

6. After reading about groundwater, hypothesise about the possibility of a **well** going dry. Why would this happen? Could it have water again?

7. Record breakers! What is the name and where is the location of ...
   a. the longest river in the world?
   b. the largest river?
   c. the highest lake?
   d. the largest group of lakes?
   e. the largest lake in the world?
   f. the largest ocean?

8. Use an atlas to help you locate the following bodies of water around the world. Where you would have to be if you were ...
   a. fishing at the source of the Nile river?
   b. bathing in the mouth of the Volga river?
   c. about to dock at a port in the East of India?
   d. paddling up the longest river in the United States?
   e. in the mouth of a river between two countries in South America?
   f. visiting a sacred river for Hindus?
   g. studying icebergs between Russia and Alaska?
   h. snorkelling in a south Jamaican beach?
   i. surfing in west New Zealand?
   j. making a crossing between Egypt and Saudi Arabia?

9. This is a list of the longest rivers in the world in descending order. Look at the map on page 75 and locate them all.
   a. Nile
   b. Amazon
   c. Yangtze
   d. Mississippi
   e. Yenisei
   f. Huang He
   g. Ob
   h. Paraná
   i. Congo
   j. Amur
   k. Lena
   l. Mekong

   Then, copy and complete the following chart in your notebook:

Contient	America	Europe	Africa	Asia	Oceania
Longest river	Mississipi				

10 Read the following text and answer the questions below:

> "The Three Gorges Dam in the Yangtze River (China) was completed in 2012. It is the largest hydroelectric dam in the world. It was built for a variety of purposes including irrigation, flood control and as a means of producing electricity. The Chinese government saw this as a way of reducing the emission of greenhouse gases by developing hydroelectric power and relying less on coal and other fossil fuels. The dam could also be used to increase trade and navigation between distant regions in China, as well as improving water shortage problems. However, the project has been shrouded in controversy. To start with, development of the dam led to the relocation of more than one million people. There are also environmental concerns because of altered weather patterns, landslides, and the effect on the surrounding ecology. Additionally, the dam has left many important archaeological and cultural sites covered by water."

a. Why does the author of the text say the project has been 'shrouded in controversy'?
b. In your own words, make a list of the pros and cons of the dam.
c. Would you consider the change in landscape that this project has caused to be a problem? Why or why not?
d. What impact has this dam had? Would you say it has been a good or a bad project? Who has it been good or bad for?

11 Think back to what you've just studied about rivers in the Mediterranean watershed. Then, using this information, write a report on Almería and its dependence on aquifers for drinking water.

12 Which countries do the Rhine and the Danube pass through? Use an atlas or the Internet to find out.

13 What are the largest lakes in Europe? What are their input sources?

14 Read about the distribution of rivers in Africa again. How have they affected human settlement?

15 What is the relationship between the multiple islands that make up Oceania and its lack of large rivers and lakes?

16 Which regions in the world have the greatest number of rivers?

17 Investigating rivers. In groups or individually, choose a river from the list in Activity 9. You are going to become an expert on that river, so get ready to present your results to the class in the form of a poster, or by using Prezi or PowerPoint. You should include information on the following: location, how long it is, land use around it (industry, farming, transportation, leisure activities ...), major cities along it, important tributaries, climate along it, and any other interesting facts. Add photographs!

18 What resources do humans obtain from rivers? And from seas and oceans?

19 In some places, water is becoming a rare resource and is often polluted. In others, there is no limit to its supply. As a class, discuss the uses of water in your community.

a. Make a list with all the possible uses of water.
b. Do you use water in any of the ways mentioned in the previous activity? Select the uses from your list.
c. What are the environmental impacts for each of these uses? What are some ways of reducing these impacts? Is there anything you personally can do about it?

Read and think

WHY ARE CLOUDS SOMETIMES WHITE AND SOMETIMES GREY?

Clouds are made up of millions of tiny droplets of water and ice crystals which scatter the Sun's light in all directions. When these drops and crystals are exactly the right size, they reflect all the visible colours that hit them and the cloud looks white.

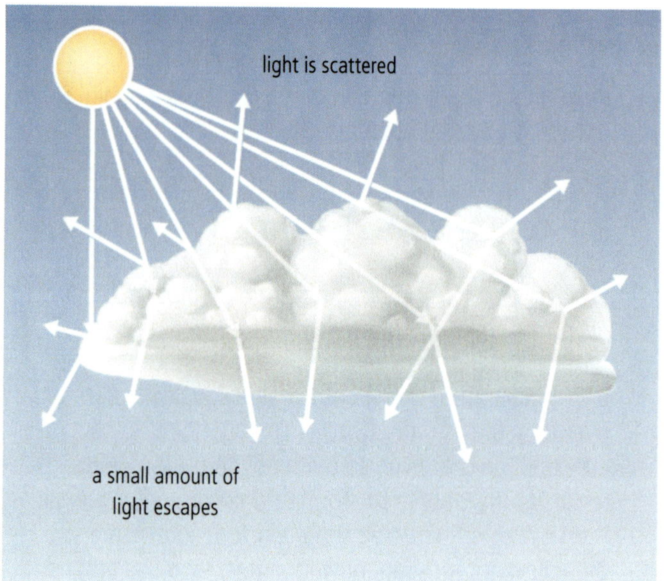

The brightness of a cloud depends on how much of the Sun's light is reflected from the cloud. If the cloud is thin, there are fewer water particles to scatter the light, so the cloud will not look bright white. However, the sides of clouds are often very bright because a lot of light is scattered out of the sides. If a cloud is very thick, only a small amount of light escapes out of the bottom of the cloud, so the base looks grey.

Clouds also look grey because of shadows: sometimes because they are in the shadow of other clouds and sometimes because of their own shadow. Consequently, when clouds cover most of the sky, as they often do in the United Kingdom, they look grey because they are blocking out most of the sunlight!

Storm clouds (cumulonimbus) are sometimes so thick that sunlight cannot pass through them. This is why they appear black. However, if you view the same cloud from above, you will see that it is, in fact, still predominantly white. It is only the base of the cloud that receives no light.

Next time you see a cloud, take a closer look!

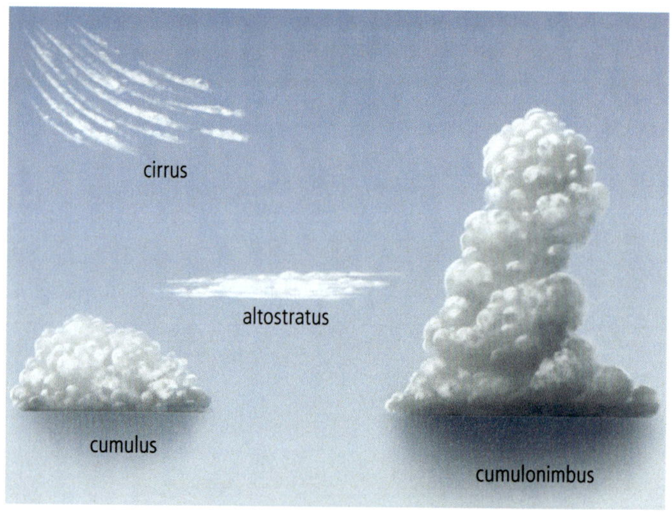

ANSWER THE QUESTIONS

1. Answer the questions.

- **a.** What are clouds made of?
- **b.** Why don't thin clouds look bright white?
- **c.** Why does the bottom of a thick cloud look grey?
- **d.** Why do storm clouds look black?

2. Find words in the text that mean the following:

- **a.** very small drops
- **b.** diffuse
- **c.** appear
- **d.** brilliance

3. How are clouds formed?

4. When and how does rain occur?

5. What clouds can be associated with the *gota fría* (cold front) phenomenon? Why?

Work it out

CONCEPT MAP

Use the words in the word cloud to create your own unit map in your notebook. Write any connecting texts you need.

Arctic Ocean Europe Atlantic Ocean salt water liquid

gas seas and oceans fresh water Cantabrian Sea

large flow groundwater Indian Ocean

watershed lakes **The hydrosphere** Spain

Atlantic Ocean surface water

Black Sea Caspian Sea rivers America Asia

Africa Mediterranean Sea long

distribution of water

Pacific Ocean short inland water solid glaciers

SELF-ASSESSMENT

Carry out a self-assessment of what you have learnt in this unit. Choose one answer for each question and then check your answers.

1. Most liquid water on our planet is …
   a. groundwater
   b. seawater
   c. fresh water
2. What is the most common component of seawater?
   a. Magnesium salts.
   b. Magnesium chloride.
   c. Sodium chloride.
3. The water in a river has a powerful erosive force in the …
   a. upper course.
   b. middle course.
   c. lower course.
4. What is a lagoon?
   a. A seasonal lake.
   b. An underground lake.
   c. A lake that forms on coastlines.
5. Groundwater accumulates from …
   a. seawater
   b. rainwater
   c. ice
6. Glaciers erode the landscape and form …
   a. moraines.
   b. U-shaped valleys.
   c. V-shaped valleys.
7. Most rivers on the Iberian Peninsula empty into …
   a. the Cantabrian Sea.
   b. the Atlantic Ocean.
   c. the Mediterranean Sea.
8. The longest river on the Peninsula is the …
   a. Tajo
   b. Duero
   c. Guadalquivir
9. Which river is one of Europe's most important transport routes?
   a. The Oder.
   b. The Rhône.
   c. The Rhine.
10. The deepest fresh water lake on Earth is …
    a. Lake Ladoga, Europe.
    b. Lake Titicaca, South America.
    c. Lake Baikal, Asia.

05 Atmosphere: Weather and climate

<< LOOKING BACK

- What is the atmosphere composed of?
- How do clouds form?
- Look at image C. What is a hurricane?
- What types of climate do you know?
- Where are the coldest places on Earth?
- What is the weather like where you live?

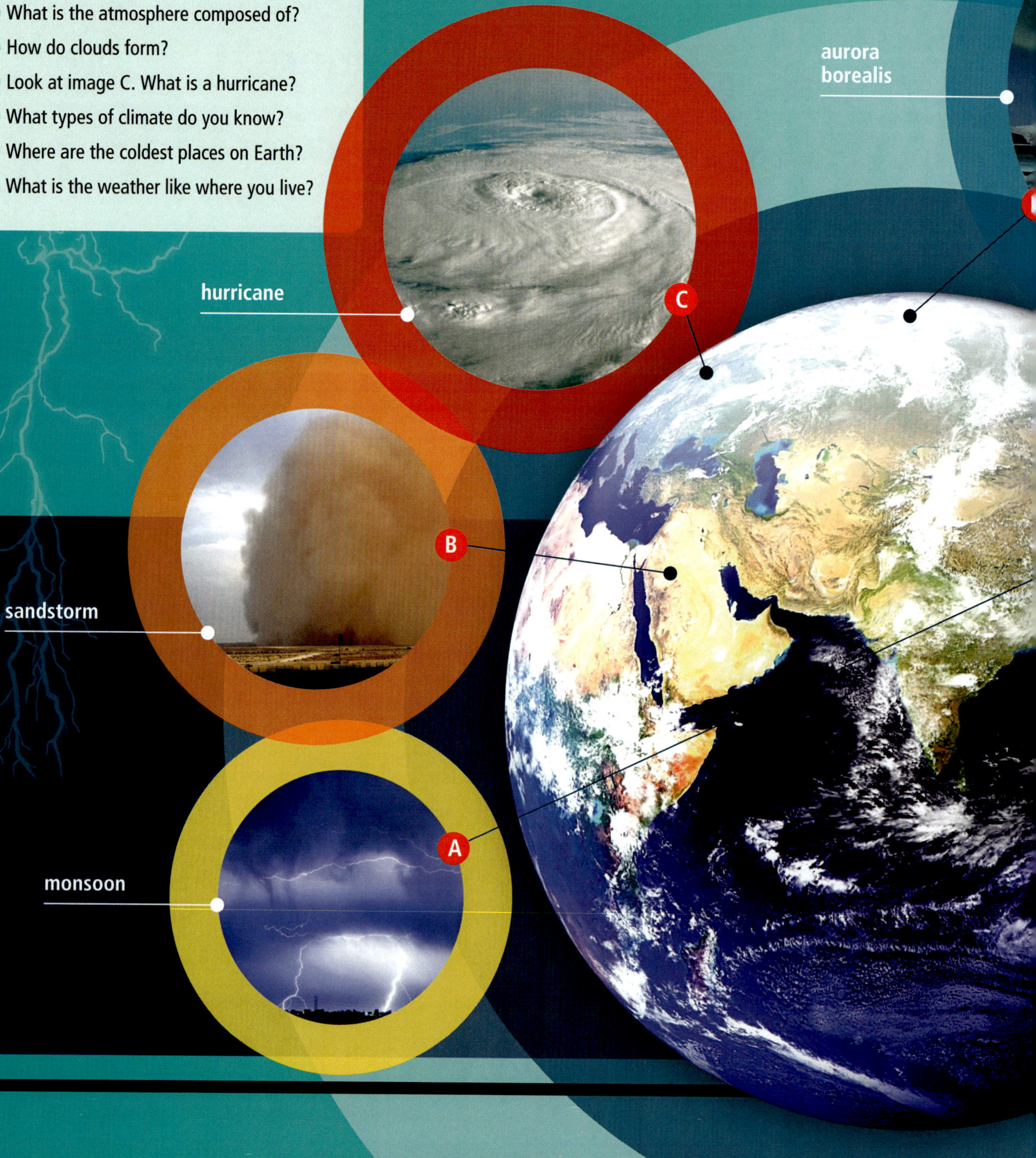

It's raining cats and dogs…

That is what English speakers sometimes say when it is raining very heavily but there is no historical evidence that this has ever really happened! However, for centuries there have been reports of smaller animals, such as fish and frogs, falling from the sky.

Two weather phenomena may be responsible for this. The first theory involves waterspouts. A waterspout is a tornado that forms over land and travels over water. The vortex at the centre of the waterspout is strong enough to suck up surrounding air, water, and small objects. These objects are deposited on the earth as 'rain' when the waterspout loses its energy.

The second theory involves updrafts. An updraft is a wind current caused by warm air from high pressure areas near the earth rising into cooler, low-pressure areas in the atmosphere. Updrafts can pick up light debris and carry it for long distances. Consequently, this could be another explanation for animals falling from the sky.

The question is: Why does it 'rain' only frogs or only fish?

- What is the difference between a tornado and a waterspout?
- What meteorological phenomenon occurs when warm air rises and cools quickly?

LOOKING FORWARD >>

- Has the Earth's atmosphere always been the same?
- How does temperature affect the amount of water vapour that air can hold?
- What is the difference between weather and climate?
- What factors affect climate?
- In which climate zone is Europe located?
- Which part of Spain has a subtropical climate?
- How can be used a climograph to determine which hemisphere an area is in?

1 The Earth's atmosphere

Has the Earth's atmosphere always been the same?

The Earth's atmosphere is a protective layer of gas that surrounds the planet. The atmosphere begins on the planet's surface and is structured in layers that have different temperature conditions and gas compositions. The atmosphere reaches an altitude of approximately 10 000 km.

DID YOU KNOW?

The Earth's atmosphere began to form around 600 million years ago from volcanic gases. It was mainly composed of carbon dioxide with little to no oxygen. The atmospheres of Mars and Venus are believed to be similar to Earth's early atmosphere.

The outermost layer of atmosphere is called the **exosphere**. It extends to the highest limits of the atmosphere where only molecules of helium and hydrogen are found.

The temperature in the exosphere varies greatly between thousands of degrees in the daytime and falling to -273.15 °C at night!

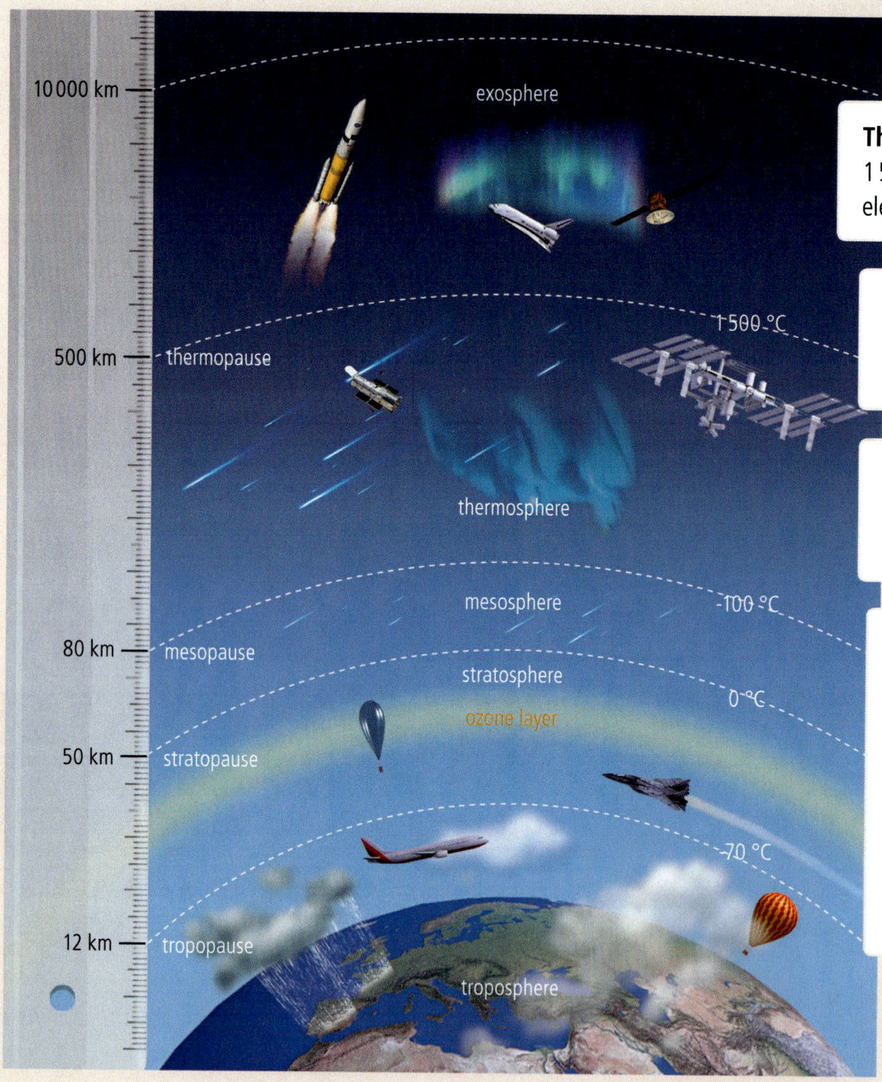

Thermosphere temperatures reach up to 1 500 °C, where solar radiation produces electrically-charged, ionised gases.

Temperatures in the **mesosphere** decrease as altitude increases. They sometimes reach -100 °C.

The ozone layer is found in the middle of the **stratosphere**. This layer absorbs ultraviolet radiation and has very high temperatures.

Almost all water vapour and 80% of the atmosphere's gases are contained in the lowest level, the **troposphere**, which is in contact with the surface of the Earth. The high content of gas and water vapour mean that most **meteorological phenomena**, such as cloud formation, wind, and rain occur at this level. Here temperatures drop by 0.65 °C for every 100 m of altitude.

Layers of the atmosphere

ACTIVITIES

1. Which layer would you associate most closely to climate and weather?
2. What is the lowest possible temperature in the atmosphere? How does this compare to the lowest temperatures on the Earth's surface? What does this tell you about the importance of the atmosphere?

2 The properties of air

How does temperature affect the amount of water vapour that air can hold?

The atmosphere is composed of air. Air is matter; it has mass, temperature and pressure. These are the most important properties of air:

COMPOSITION OF GASES

Air is a mixture of gases: 78% **nitrogen**, 21% **oxygen** and various other components such as water vapour.

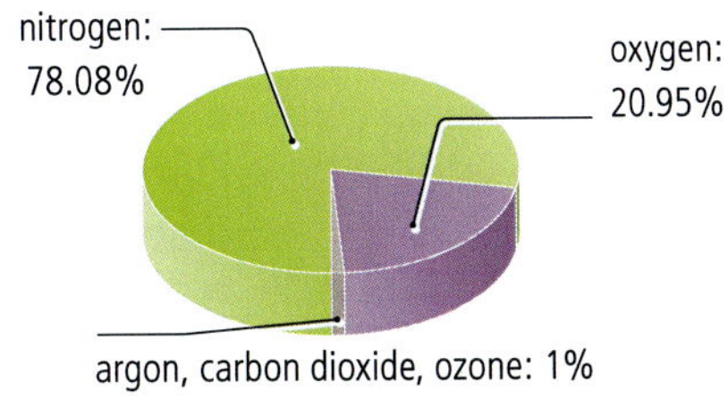

TEMPERATURE

The properties of air are affected by heat from the Earth's surface. When air is heated it expands, becomes lighter and rises. Air temperature becomes colder as it gets further from the Earth's surface. When it is cooler, the air begins to fall back towards the surface. This process only occurs within the lowest atmospheric level: the troposphere.

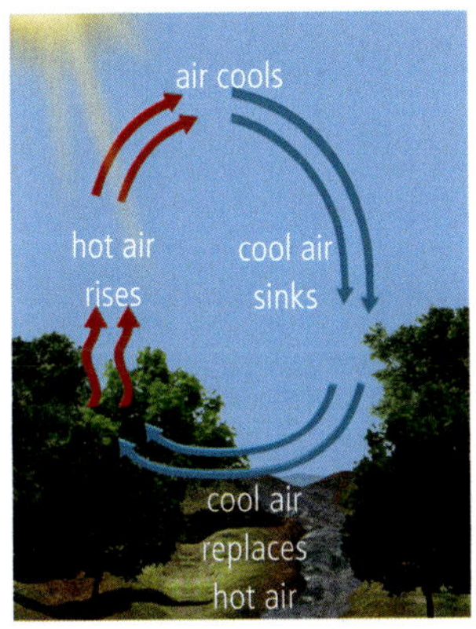

ATMOSPHERIC PRESSURE

The gases in air have weight that presses down on the Earth's surface. Atmospheric pressure is the term used to describe the pressure **exerted** on Earth by the weight of the air. It is measured with a barometer.

Both **altitude** and **temperature** determine atmospheric pressure.

RELATIVE HUMIDITY

- The amount of water vapour in the air is variable.
- Relative humidity refers to the amount of water vapour that air contains.
- Warmer air can hold more water vapour, but **all air temperatures have a maximum amount of water vapour**.
- If the maximum is **exceeded**, the vapour begins to condense into droplets and **clouds are formed**.

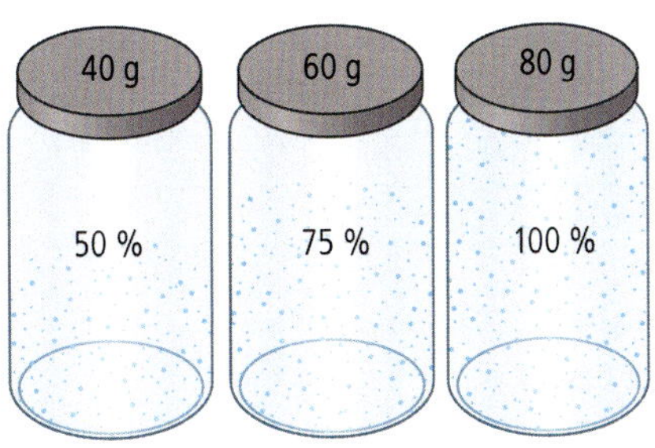

If one litre of air contains 40 g of water vapour and the maximum it can hold is 80 g, the relative humidity is 50%.

BIG THINKER

Emilio Herrera was a Spanish engineer, scientist, pilot and politician. After studying the upper layers of the atmosphere, in 1933 he designed a suit that would enable people to fly at 22 000 metres in an open balloon. This suit was the model for the spacesuits later designed by NASA for its astronauts.

ACTIVITIES

3. Which gas forms the largest component of air? What percentage does it make up?
4. What happens when the maximum amount of water vapour in the air is exceeded?
5. What two factors dictate atmospheric pressure? Do we feel the effects of a change in atmospheric pressure if we fly in an aeroplane? Explain your answer.

3 Atmospheric dynamics

What is the difference between weather and climate?

3.1 Weather and climate

The Sun's rays **warm up** the atmosphere and our planet's surface. The energy from the Sun is responsible for the Earth's weather and climate.

Weather is the state of the lower layers of the atmosphere at a certain time and place on Earth.

Meteorology is the study of the atmosphere and the atmospheric phenomena that affect weather.

Climate refers to the state of the weather in a certain region of the planet over a long period of time.

Climatology is the study of climate.

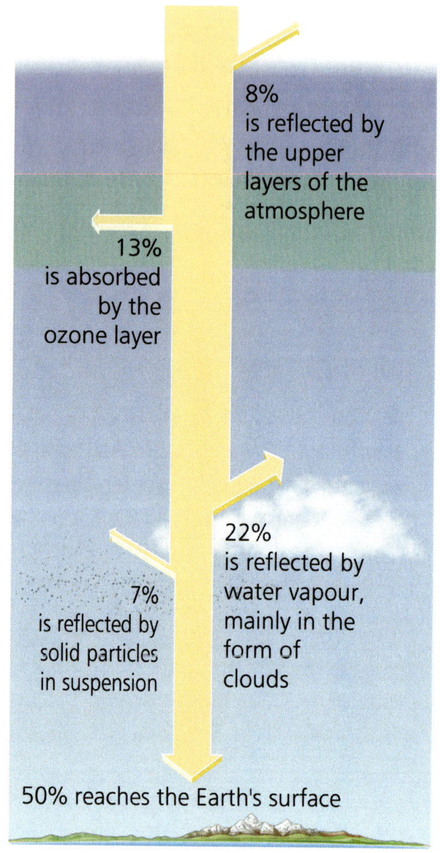

Effect of the atmosphere on the solar radiation reaching the Earth's surface.

3.2 Factors that influence weather

Weather can be determined by many different factors, such as atmospheric pressure, temperature, wind, humidity and precipitation.

ATMOSPHERIC PRESSURE

Atmospheric pressure is measured in hPa (**hectopascals**). Atmospheric pressure varies from one place to another and depends on:

Altitude: atmospheric pressure is lower at higher altitudes. For example, the amount of air at the top of a mountain is less than at the base.

Temperature: warm air weighs less than cold air. As a result, warm air rises and exerts less pressure on the Earth's surface while cold air descends and exerts more pressure.

Weather map

Anticyclones (H) are areas of high pressure (more than 1013 hPa). They form when a mass of cold air descends and the pressure increases. They produce **stable** weather.

Depressions (L) are areas of low pressure (less than 1013 hPa). They form when a mass of warm air rises and the pressure decreases. They produce **unstable** weather.

ACTIVITIES

6. Is there an anticyclone or a depression in the following situations?
   - It has been raining all day long.
   - Tomorrow will be very cold and sunny.
7. Look at the diagram above. What part of the energy of the Sun reaches the Earth's surface?
8. Going by what you've read, which phenomena do you think can help explain why it is more difficult to breath in higher altitudes?

TEMPERATURE

Temperature is measured in degrees on the Fahrenheit (°F) or Celsius (°C) scales. Temperature varies according to altitude, latitude, and distance from the sea.

Altitude: temperature decreases with elevation. This is because the surface is warmed up by the Sun and in turn it warms up the air around it.

Latitude: because the Earth is spherical, only the area near the Equator receives direct sunlight. So, the farther away from the Equator (or the higher the latitude) the colder it gets.

Distance from the sea: water heats and cools down more slowly than the land does. This explains why the temperature of the land near large bodies of water is often **milder**, with no big variations in temperature.

WIND

Masses of air move around in the atmosphere: this movement causes wind. Air always moves from areas of high pressure to areas of low pressure. Depending on the source of the winds, they are dry or bring rain, and they influence temperature.

There are different types of wind:

Prevailing winds, such as **trade winds**, always blow in the same direction and in the same regions.

Periodic winds, such as monsoons vary depending on the season.

Local winds are found in small areas. They usually blow in the same direction. Some examples in Spain are Tramontana (Islas Baleares), Galerna (Cantabrian Sea) and Cierzo (Aragón).

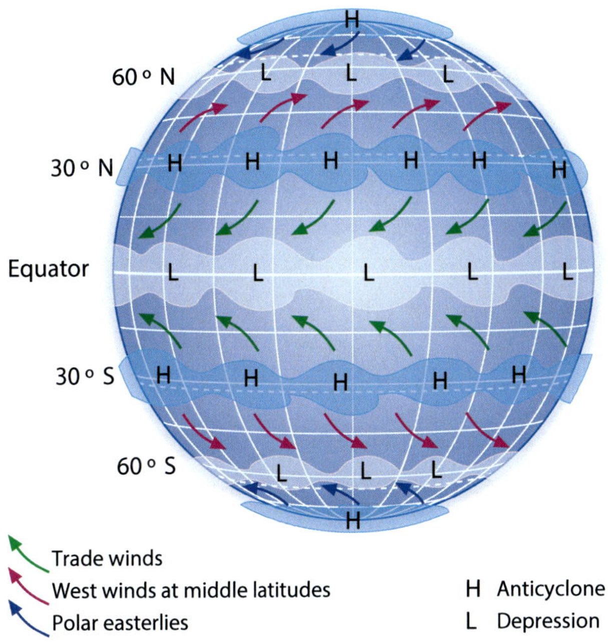

Global winds

HUMIDITY AND PRECIPITATION

All air masses contain a certain amount of water vapour or **atmospheric humidity**. As a mass of warm air rises, its temperature decreases. The humidity it contains is transformed into a liquid state and falls to the Earth's surface in the form of precipitation. There are three main causes of precipitation:

Frontal rainfall occurs when a mass of warm, humid air comes into contact with a mass of cold air. The area of contact is a front.

Storms occur when the Sun's rays heat a mass of air. The air rises and cools quickly producing intense rain.

Relief rainfall occurs when a mass of warm air comes into contact with mountainous relief. The air rises, the temperature decreases and it rains.

ACTIVITIES

9. Why do the poles receive less sunlight than the Equator?
10. Which two factors (pressure, temperature, wind, humidity and precipitation) are affected by mountains? How?
11. Look at a globe. What type of winds helped Columbus arrive in the Americas?

4 The Earth's climates

What factors affect climate?

Climatologists divide the Earth into different climate zones. This division is based on similar temperatures and precipitation across large areas.

4.1 The Earth's climate zones

On the basis of annual temperatures we can identify three major climate zones: hot, **temperate** and **cold**. These zones coincide with the Earth's latitudes.

COLD ZONES

There are **two cold climate** zones located within the polar circles:

- One in the Northern hemisphere, made up of the Arctic Ocean, Greenland and the northern coasts of Asia, Europe and America.
- One in the Southern hemisphere, made up of the Antarctic.

In these zones, there is very little sunshine and annual average temperatures are below 0 °C.

DID YOU KNOW?

Temperatures are normally measured in the air, i.e. 1.5 metres above the ground, and not in direct sunlight. Since temperature records have existed, the highest temperature recorded was 56.7 °C in Death Valley, California, USA. The lowest temperature ever recorded was at the Vostok Station in Antarctica: – 89.2 °C!

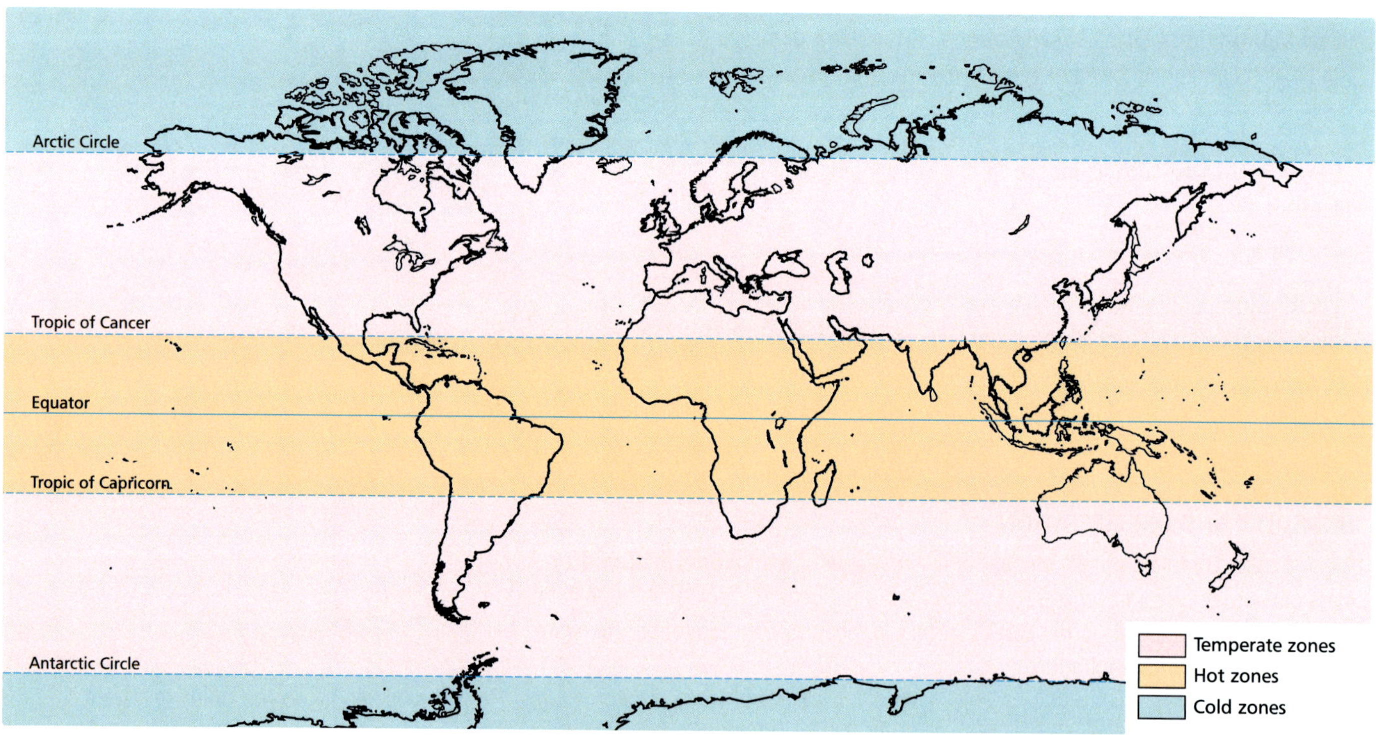

ACTIVITIES

12. Why do the North and South Poles receive so little solar energy? Read the previous page again if you need to.
13. In which continents are the cold zones found?
14. Think back to what you have learned about the factors that affect weather and climate. Then, decide whether the North Pole or the South Pole is colder. How do you know?

HOT ZONES

There is a single hot climate zone, which is known as the intertropical zone. It is situated between the two tropics.

The intense sunshine in this region produces annual average temperatures of above 18 °C.

TEMPERATE ZONES

There are two temperate climate zones which are located between the tropics and the polar circles. In these regions, annual average temperatures are between 0 °C and 18 °C.

The amount of sunshine varies throughout the year, resulting in four seasons. In the Northern hemisphere, the hot season coincides with the summer months. In the Southern hemisphere, it coincides with the winter months.

Within climate zones there are regions with different types of climate. Climatologists use the annual precipitation recorded in these regions to further distinguish between the different climates.

PRECIPITATION
Rainy climate: More than 800 l/m^2 per year
Intermediate climate: 300-800 l/m^2 per year
Dry climate: Less than 300 l/m^2 per year

SEASONS AND TREES

Trees are adapted to the climate of the area in which they grow. Some trees lose their leaves once a year to adapt to the differences in temperature and light that occur as the seasons change. This adaptation allows trees to conserve energy and protect themselves from any damage. Trees that lose all their leaves at the same time are called **deciduous**; whereas trees that have leaves throughout the year are called **evergreens**.

ACTIVITIES

15. What is the difference between climates that exist in the same climate area?

16. Copy and complete the chart in your notebook:

Climate zone	Average annual temperature

17. What makes a climate dry?

18. Which of the three climate zones has four **distinct** seasons in relation to temperature?

19. Why does the amount of solar energy vary throughout the year in the temperate zone?

4.2 The Earth's climate types

The combination of annual temperature and precipitation data results in nine different climate types.

COLD CLIMATES

Polar climate

This climate depends on latitude.

It has very low temperatures, below 0 °C.

There is very little precipitation, less than 200 l/m² per year. Precipitation is always in the form of snow.

Alpine climate

This climate depends on altitude. It is found in high mountains.

It has very cold winters and cool summers.

Precipitation is abundant, mostly in the form of snow.

HOT CLIMATES

Equatorial climate

This has high temperatures throughout the year. The annual average temperature is over 22 °C. There is abundant precipitation, sometimes more than 2 000 l/m² per year.

Tropical climate

This has high temperatures of over 22 °C.

Precipitation is abundant and is irregular throughout the year. There is a rainy season and a dry season.

Desert climate

This is extremely **arid**. Annual precipitation is less than 250 l/m². There are significant differences between temperatures during the day and at night.

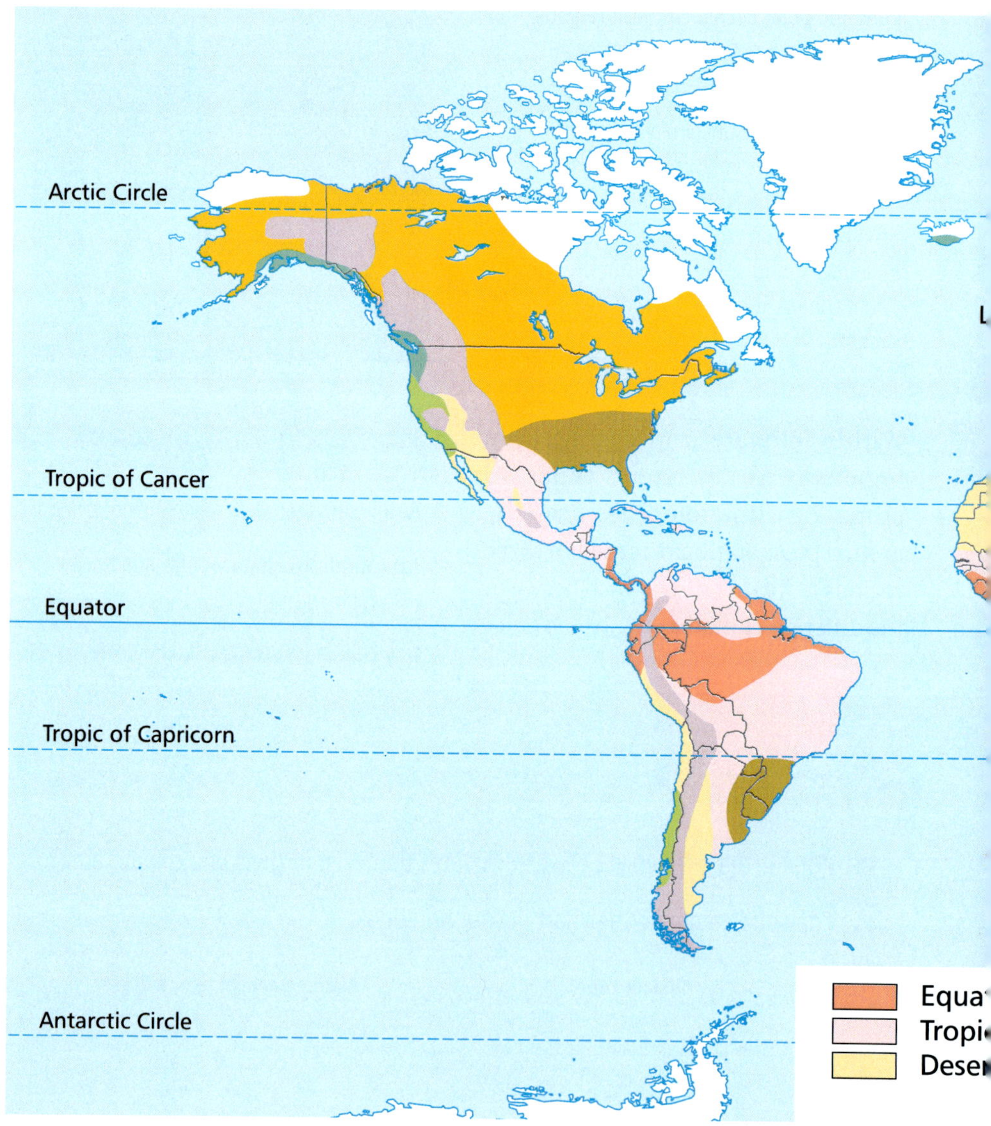

ACTIVITIES

20. Locate any alpine climates. Name the mountain range that gives rise to that climate.

21. What climates can you find in North America?

22. What is the main difference between the tropical and the equatorial climate?

TEMPERATE CLIMATES

Mediterranean climate

This has hot summers and mild winters. Average annual temperatures are between 15 °C and 20 °C.

Precipitation is low, generally less than 700 l/m² per year. It mainly occurs in autumn and spring, while summer is often dry.

Continental climate

Summers are hot and winters are cold. In some winter months, the temperature drops below 0 °C.

Precipitation is low and mainly happens during the summer.

Oceanic climate

This has mild temperatures all year round, with cool summers and mild winters.

Precipitation is abundant and regular, more than 800 l/m² per year.

Humid subtropical climate

Temperatures are high in the summer and mild during the winter.

Precipitation is abundant, more than 1 000 l/m² per year, and concentrated in the summer.

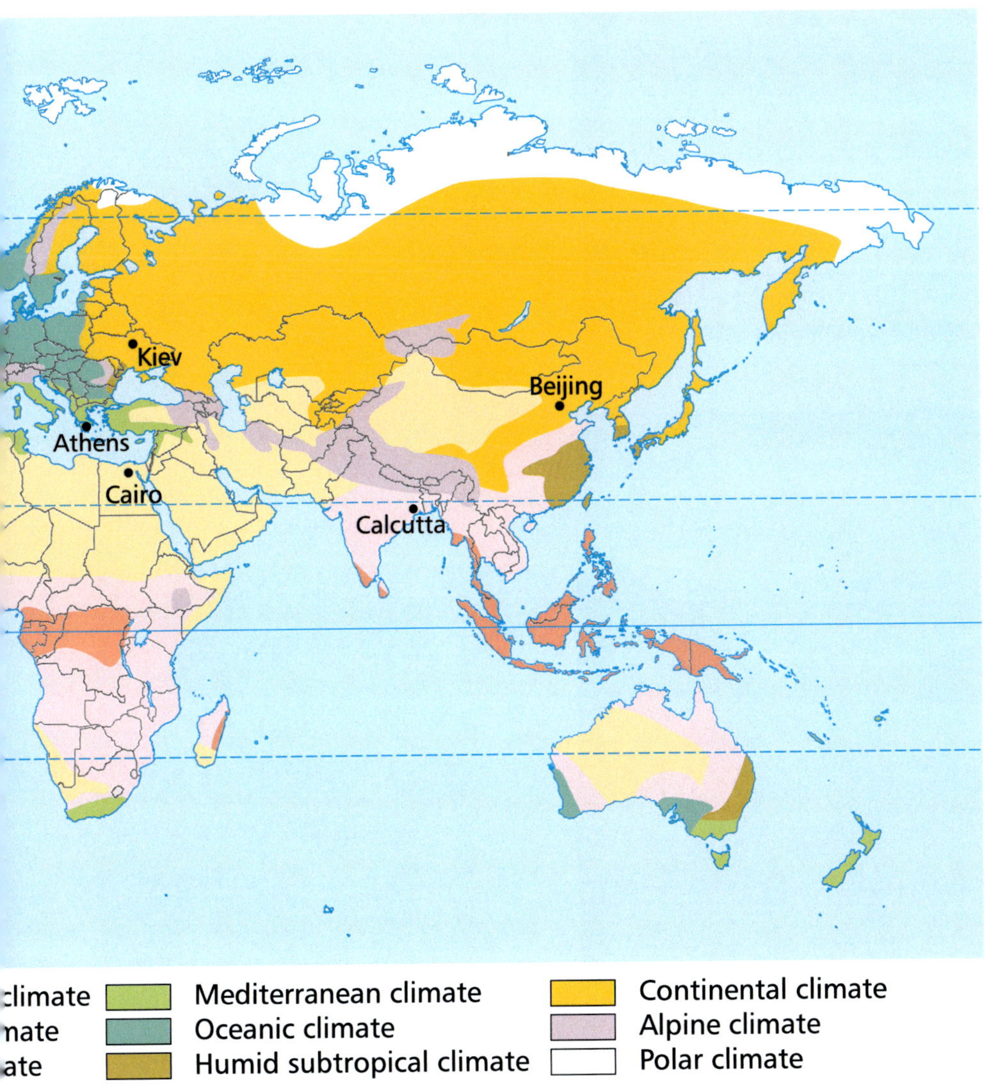

WHAT IS A CLIMOGRAPH?

Temperature and precipitation make it possible to identify a climate.

Both elements can be shown graphically using a climograph which allows us to observe the annual change in temperature and precipitation in a specific place on the planet.

This information is represented using a combination chart with two systems of **coordinates**.

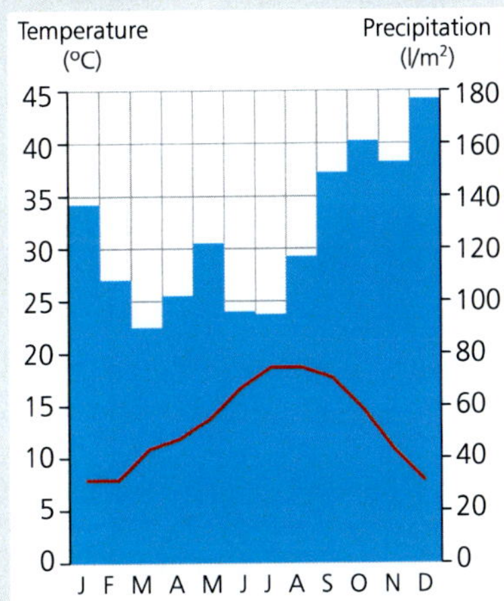

Oceanic climate

ACTIVITIES

23. Compare temperatures between Mediterranean and Oceanic climates.

24. Would you be more likely to find humid subtropical climates in eastern or western continents?

25. Which climate only exists in the Northern hemisphere? Why do you think this happens?

5 Climates in Europe

Most of Europe is in the Northern hemisphere's temperate zone. However, the northernmost regions are in the Polar circle.

POLAR CLIMATE

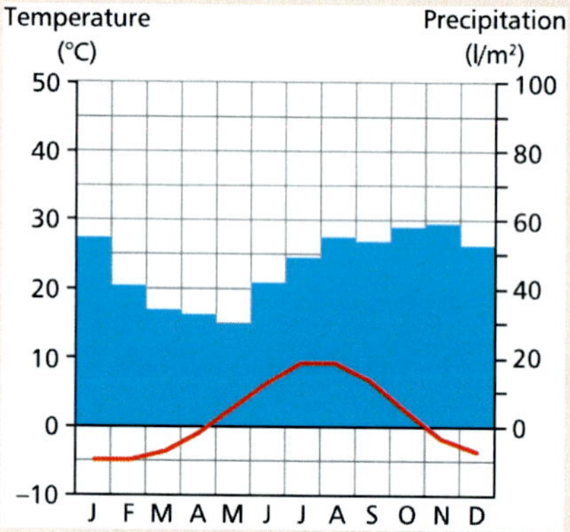

Climograph for Vardo (Norway)

This is found in northern Iceland, Norway and Russia.

ALPINE CLIMATE

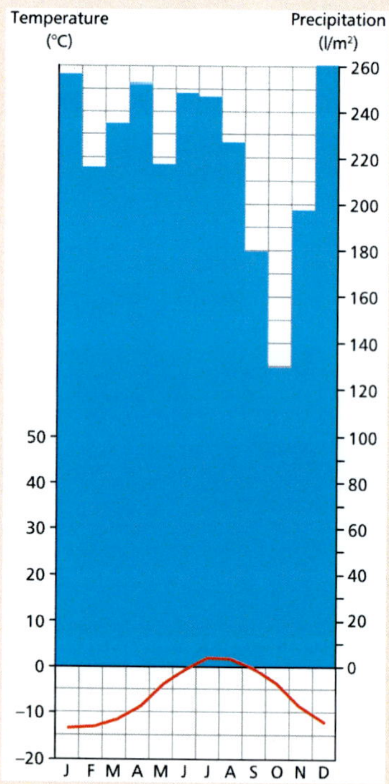

Climograph for Sonnblick (Austria)

This is characteristic of Europe's large mountain ranges, mainly the Caucasus Mountains, the Alps and the Pyrenees.

ACTIVITIES

26. Which climate predominates in northern Europe? Which one predominates in the south? And in the east?

27. Make a note of all the mountain ranges with an alpine climate.

28. Look at the map and write the names of the countries that only have one type of climate. Write the name of the climate too.

In which climate zone is Europe located?

OCEANIC CLIMATE

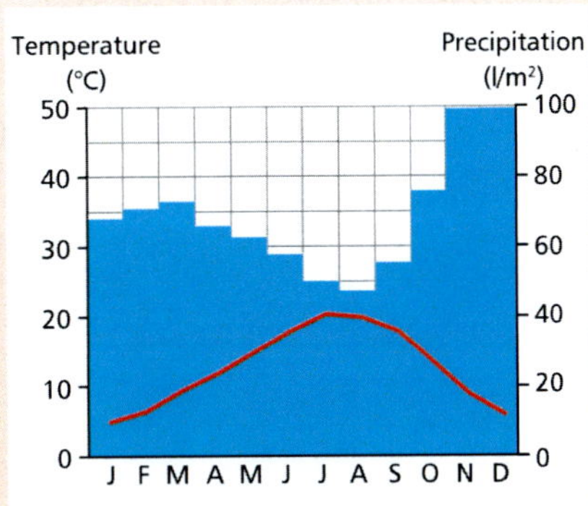

Climograph for Bordeaux (France)

This can be found along the coasts of Western Europe and the shores of the Atlantic Ocean.

CONTINENTAL CLIMATE

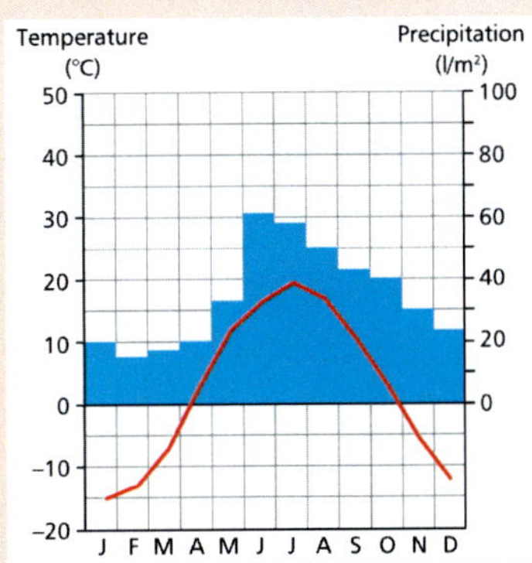

Climograph for Kazan (Russia)

This type of climate covers an area between the Russian Plain and the centre of the continent where there is no maritime influence.

MEDITERRANEAN CLIMATE

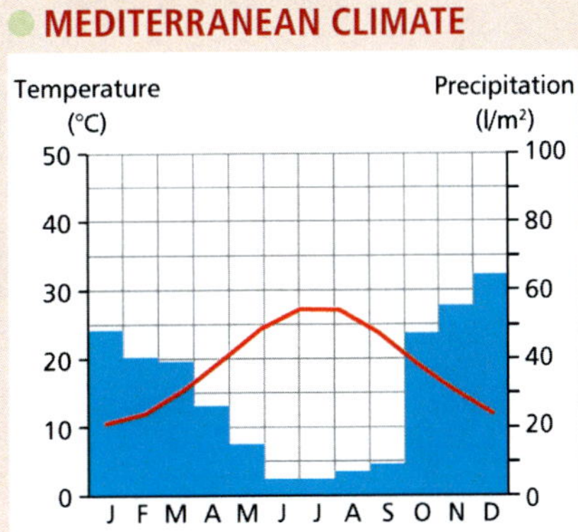

Climograph for Athens (Greece)

This climate is found along the Mediterranean coast of Europe and the Atlantic coast of the Iberian Peninsula.

29. Imagine that you were going to Moscow, Russia, by car. Plan your **itinerary** and the countries you are going to pass through. Then, identify the climates you will find during your trip.

6 Climates in Spain

Which part of Spain has a subtropical climate?

Most of the Iberian Peninsula and the Islas Baleares have a Mediterranean climate. However, there are differences between inland areas and the coastal areas.

ALPINE CLIMATE

This can be found in the Cordillera Cantábrica and the Pyrenees, and above 1 500 m. in the Sistema Ibérico, Sistema Central and Sistemas Béticos.

Asturias

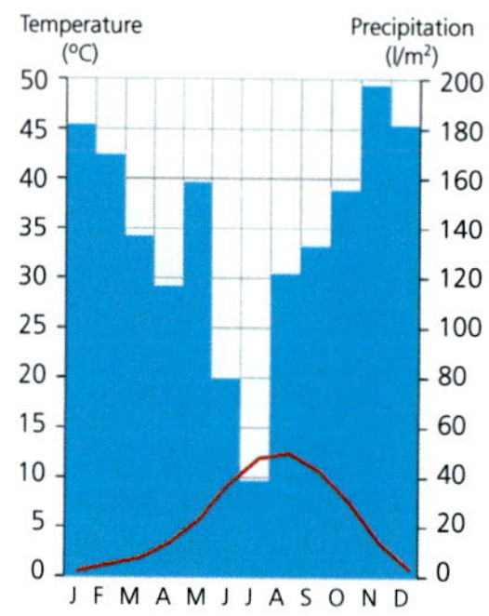

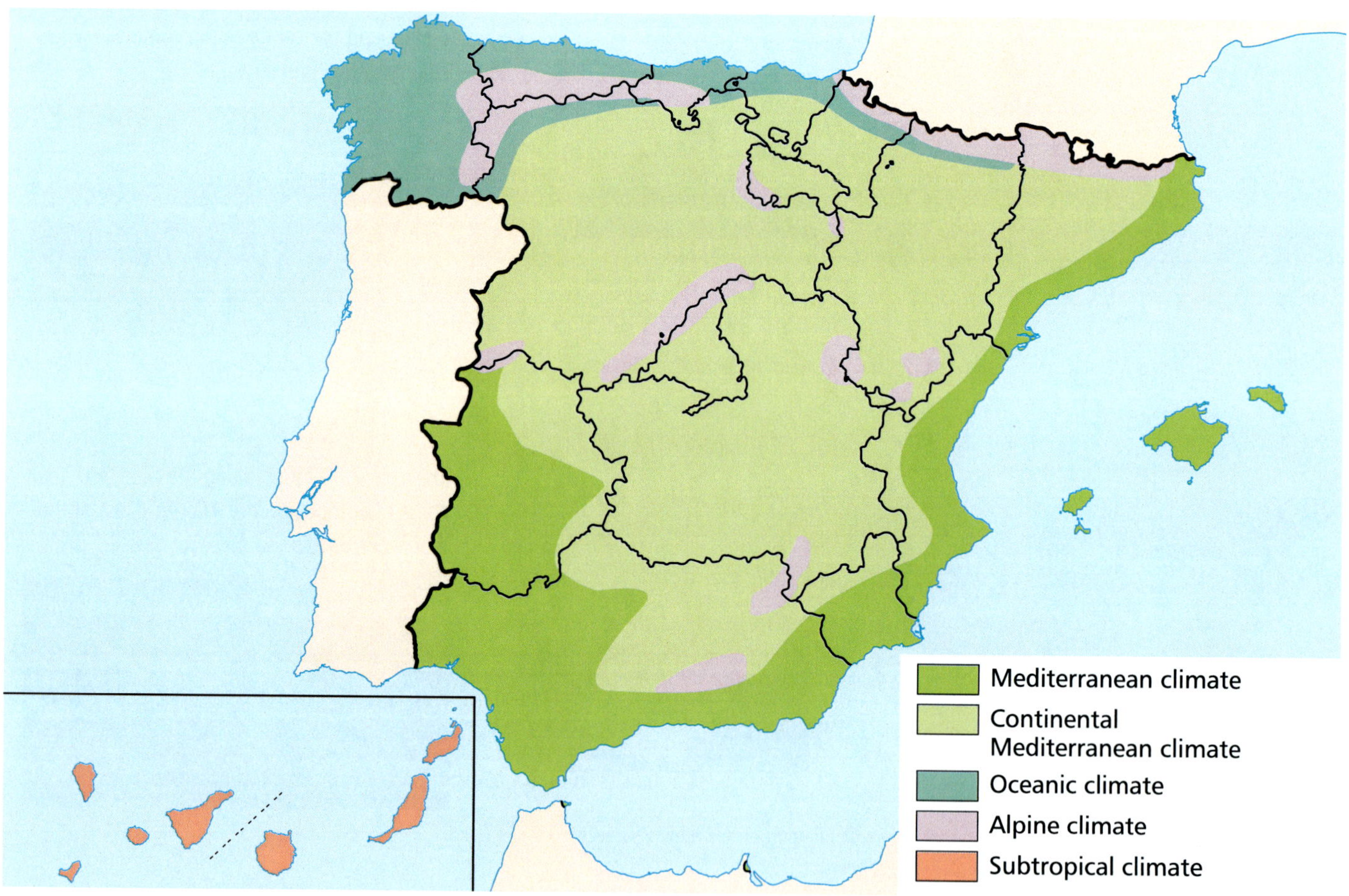

ACTIVITIES

30. Draw a line from Bilbao to Cádiz. What different climates does it pass through? What climatic factors explain those different climates?

31. Would you prefer to spend the summer in Valencia or La Coruña? Why?

32. Would you prefer to spend the winter in Bilbao or Soria? Explain your answer.

OCEANIC CLIMATE

This climate is located along the coast of Cantabria and the foot of the Pyrenees.

It has mild temperatures throughout the year. There is regular, abundant precipitation.

San Sebastián

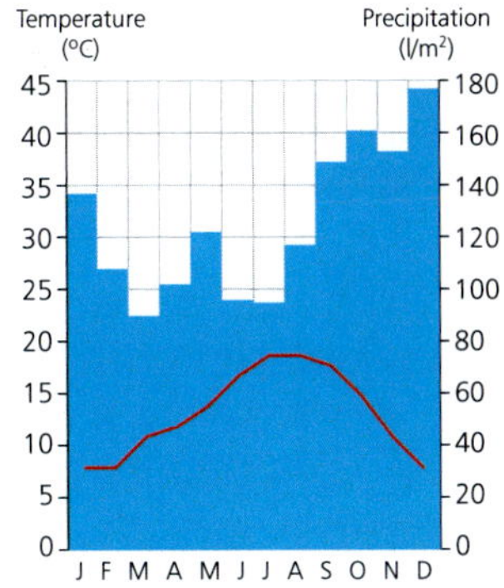

MEDITERRANEAN CLIMATE

This is located on the coast of Cataluña, Valencia, Murcia, Andalucía, on the Islas Baleares, and in Ceuta and Melilla.

Temperatures are mild. Precipitation is low and irregular. There are often droughts in the summer.

Málaga

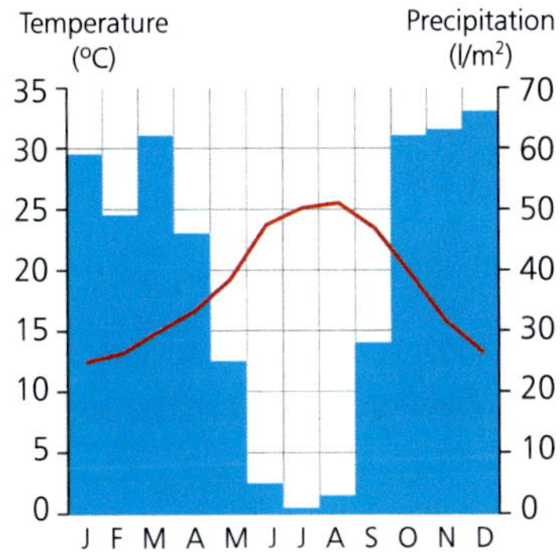

CONTINENTAL MEDITERRANEAN CLIMATE

This is located between the Meseta and the Valle del Ebro.

This climate is characterised by significant changes in temperature. The winters are cold and the summers are hot. Precipitation is low and concentrated in the spring and autumn.

Segovia

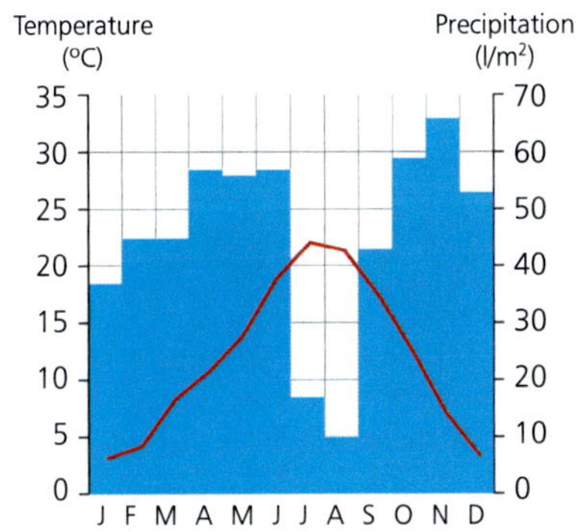

SUBTROPICAL CLIMATE

This climate is located in the Islas Canarias.

It has high temperatures all year round and little precipitation.

Las Palmas de Gran Canaria

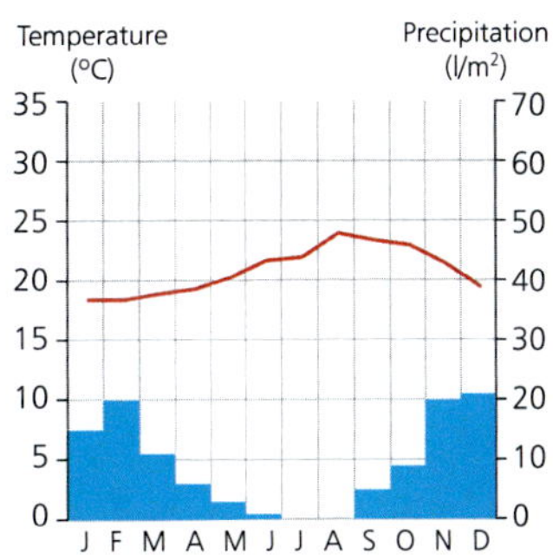

ACTIVITIES

33. What are the similarities and differences between the Mediterranean climate and the Continental Mediterranean climate?

34. Which areas in Spain receive less precipitation? Which ones receive more precipitation?

35. In what ways is climate an important resource for Spain?

Discovery techniques

MAKING AND INTERPRETING A CLIMOGRAPH

How to make a climograph

Step 1

Take a piece of graph paper and draw a horizontal line. This will be the x-axis. Divide the axis into twelve equal segments, representing the twelve months of the year, and label them using the first letters of the months.

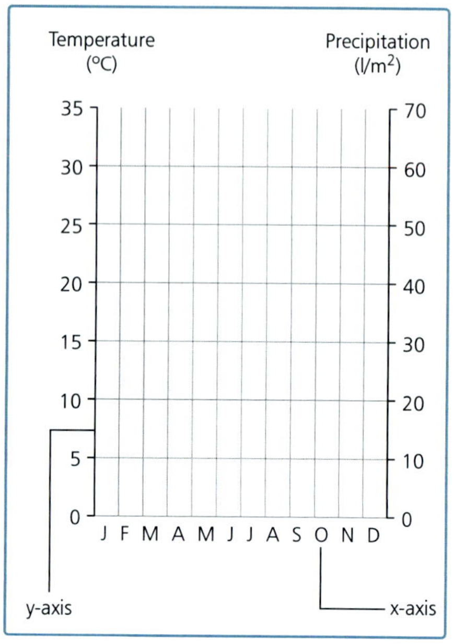

Step 2

Draw two vertical lines, one at each end of the x-axis. These will be the y-axes.

- The left-hand line will be used to indicate temperature. Divide it into 5 °C segments and label them up to 35 °C.

  If you need to show values below zero, extend the axis below the x-axis.

- The right-hand line will indicate precipitation. Divide it into 10 l/m² segments and label them. The figures on this axis are usually twice those on the temperature axis.

Step 3

You will need to obtain data from a weather station. In this example, the data is from a weather station in Alicante.

Alicante	Jan	Feb	Mar	Apr	May	Jun	Jul	Aug	Sep	Oct	Nov	Dec	Average Total
T °C	11.5	12.4	13.7	15.5	18.4	22.2	24.9	25.5	23.1	19.1	15.2	12.5	17.8
P l/m²	22	226	26	30	33	17	6	8	47	52	42	26	336

Next, **plot** the information on the graph:

- Temperature is shown by putting a dot in the appopriate month. This dot represents degrees centigrade. When you have plotted all 12 months, connect the twelve dots with a red line.

- Precipitation is shown by drawing bars in the appopriate month. The bars represent the amount of l/m². Then, colour them in blue.

  Finally, indicate the name of the weather station and write the average annual temperature and total annual precipitation.

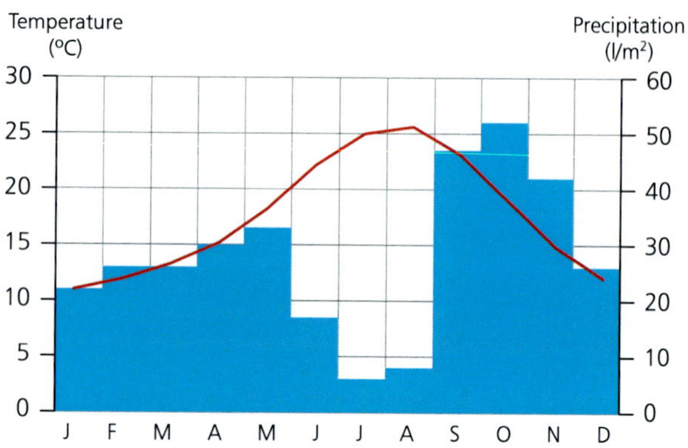

How can be used a climograph to determine which hemisphere an area is in?

Interpreting a climograph

When analysing a climograph, we need to identify the type of climate shown on the graph and determine whether there are any local variations which differentiate it from the general characteristics of that climate.

We need to look at the following elements:

1. Temperature

- **Maximum and minimum temperatures** indicate the existence of cold seasons and hot seasons. These figures help us determine the hemisphere. They also enable us to determine the **temperature range**, which is the difference in temperature between the hottest and the coldest months. If the temperature range is small, we are most likely close to the Equator or close to a large body of water.
- **Annual average temperature** allows us to relate the climograph to the major climate zones based on temperature.

2. Precipitation

- **Annual distribution of precipitation** indicates if precipitation is distributed evenly throughout the year or if there are differences between rainy seasons and dry seasons.
- **Total of precipitations** allows us to determine if the climate is wet or dry.

Climograph for Alicante

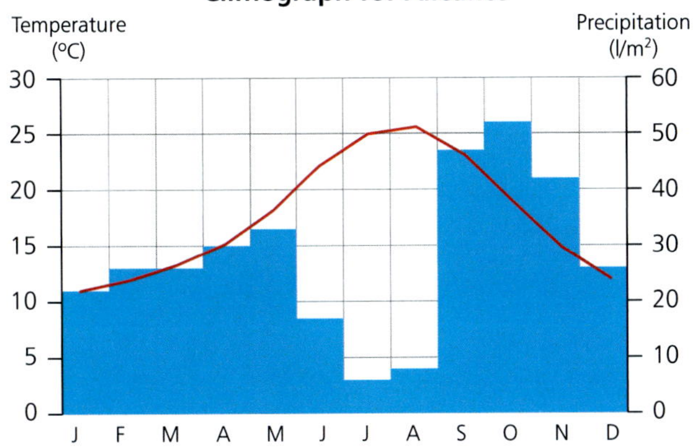

Mediterranean climate

Analysing the climograph for Alicante, for example, would allow us to reach the following conclusions:

1. The temperature data and temperature range show two distinct seasons and two intermediate seasons. In addition, the annual average temperature is typical of a temperate climate.
2. The precipitation is mainly in spring, autumn and, to a lesser extent, in winter. The driest period is in summer. This data enables us to deduce that this is a temperate climate: specifically, a Mediterranean climate.

PRACTISE WHAT YOU'VE LEARNT

1. Make two climographs using the following climate data and explain each one, identifying the climate in each place.

Baghdad	Jan	Feb	Mar	Apr	May	Jun	Jul	Aug	Sep	Oct	Nov	Dec	Average Total
T °C	9.5	12	16	21.5	27	32	35	34.5	31.2	26.5	17	11.5	22.8
P l/m²	30	33	33	23	5	0	0	0	0	3	20	30	177

Warsaw	Jan	Feb	Mar	Apr	May	Jun	Jul	Aug	Sep	Oct	Nov	Dec	Average Total
T °C	-3.5	-1.5	1.5	7.5	14	17	19	17.5	13.5	7.5	2	-1	7.8
P l/m²	30	28	33	38	48	66	76	74	48	41	38	38	558

Revision activities

1. Do the following situations refer to climate or weather?
   a. The weatherman said it will be a sunny day tomorrow.
   b. If it doesn't rain during the Easter holidays, we will go to the beach.
   c. It usually rains this time of year.
   d. Last winter was the coldest in 50 years.
   e. Summers in Scotland look like autumn in Spain.

2. Say which climate the following clues refer to.
   a. no rain in summer
   b. cool summers and mild winters
   c. cool summers and cold winters
   d. almost no rain
   e. rain in summer and cold winters
   f. only two seasons: a dry season and a rainy one
   g. rain during the summer and mild winters
   h. very little precipitation, in the form of snow
   i. no seasons: hot and humid all year round

3. Answer these questions in your notebook. Then, share the answers with your classmates:
   a. If stuck in a room where there is a fire, should you try to stand up to breathe better or should you stay low on the ground? Prove it with evidence from your textbook.
   b. Why are places with a Mediterranean climate popular as holiday destinations?
   c. Which side of the Cordillera Cantábrica is more likely to receive rain, the north or the south? Why?
   d. In southern Asia, monsoon winds blow southwest or northeast depending on the season. Which one brings the rainy season? Why does this happen?
   e. The North Atlantic Drift is an ocean current that brings warm and moist air. It passes the northern coast of Ireland and Great Britain, and then moves on to the coast of Norway. How does that current affect climate there? How might climates be different if the North Atlantic Drift didn't exist?
   f. How does climate affect our lives?

4. Have you ever heard of the 'snows of Kilimanjaro'? Locate the mountain on a map and explain how it is possible to have snow there.

5. In which climate zone is Spain?

6. An alpine climate has one characteristic that makes it different to others. What is it?

7. Look at a political map and determine which city is colder. Then, explain which factors are at play.
   a. Pamplona or Badajoz
   b. Copenhagen or Moscow
   c. Kathmandu or New Delhi

8. In pairs, decide how you would pack your bag if you were going on a trip this summer to …
   a. Mykonos in Greece
   b. Cork in Ireland
   c. Kolkata in India
   d. Santiago in Chile

9. Review the world's climate types. Copy and complete this table with information on climates:

Climate zones	Climate	Location	Average temperature	Average yearly precipitation
Cold	(2)			
Temperate	(5)			
Hot	(3)			

10. How do you think the existence of different climate zones affects population?

11. Name five countries that have mainly desert climates and predict what will happen to the population.

12. What are the main differences between the Mediterranean and humid subtropical climates?

13. Analyse climographs A and B. Then, in your notebook, answer the following questions for both climographs.

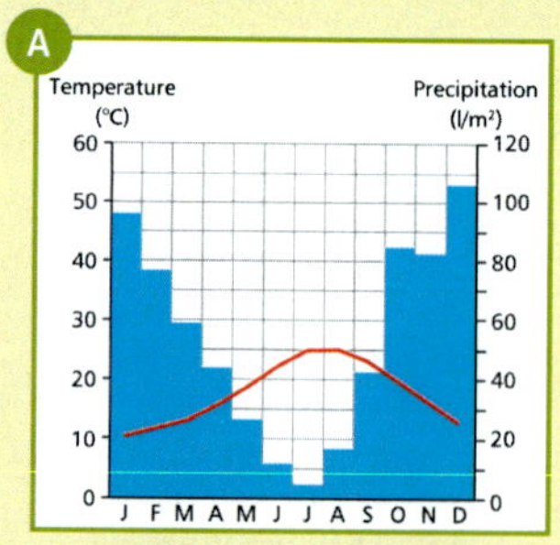

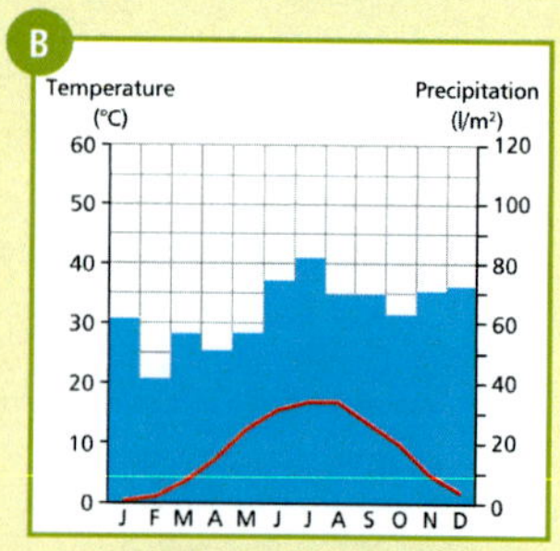

   a. Look at the temperature line. Is this climate in the Northern hemisphere or in the Southern? How can you tell?
   b. Is there a significant difference between the maximum and the minimum temperature? Going on temperature, can we see seasons?

c. What is the temperature range (highest minus lowest)? Do you think this climate is near a body of water? Why or why not?

d. Which climate zone do you think it is? Remember: T >18 °C = hot zone; T<0 °C = cold climate (T is the average temperature).

e. Look at the bars representing precipitation. Is it **evenly** distributed or not? Can we say that there is a dry season and a wet season?

f. Is precipitation very abundant, abundant, regular, scarce or practically non-existent? What does it tell you about this climate?

g. Are there any dry months? (Remember that a dry month appears when the temperature line is above the precipitation bar.)

h. What climate could this be?

14 Read the following text. Then, answer the questions using your own words and citing the text where necessary.

> "Greenhouses gases, such as carbon dioxide, trap heat in the atmosphere and regulate our climate. These gases exist naturally, but humans add more carbon dioxide by burning fossil fuels for energy (coal, oil and natural gas) and by clearing forests. Greenhouse gases act like a blanket. The thicker the blanket, the warmer our planet becomes. At the same time, the Earth's oceans are also absorbing some of this extra carbon dioxide, making them more acidic and less **hospitable** for sea life.
>
> The increase in global temperature is significantly altering our planet's climate, resulting in more extreme and unpredictable weather. Humans and wild animals face new challenges for survival because of climate change. More frequent and intense drought, storms, heat waves, rising sea levels, melting glaciers and warming oceans can directly harm animals, destroy their habitats and wreak **havoc** on people's livelihoods and communities."

Source: http://www.worldwildlife.org/

a. Write a title for this text.

b. In what way is climate changing?

c. How is this affecting the oceans?

d. What are the causes of this change?

e. What are the consequences for people?

f. What can be done to prevent climate change getting worse? Is there something you can do?

15 Locate the following cities and identify the country they belong to. Which climate does each city have?

- Moscow
- Kolkata
- Buenos Aires
- Denver
- Ouagadougou

16 Match the following weather forecast to the correct city in Activity 15.

Weather forecast for March 15th:

Average daily temperature will be 28 °C with a high of 32 °C during ***peak*** *hours. Temperatures will rise and it will be cloudier by the end of the week. Expect a heavy thunderstorm today as the rainy season approaches.*

17 These photographs belong to different climates in Spain.

a. Describe each picture and compare them.

b. Try to identify the climate. What are the clues that help you?

Read and think

THE *GOTA FRÍA*

Foreign visitors from the north of Europe come to Spain in their thousands to enjoy the sunshine and warm temperatures of the Mediterranean Sea. They sunbathe on the beaches of Valencia, Alicante or Castellón, **blissfully** unaware of the fact that heavy rainfall can be a serious problem in Mediterranean coastal regions. They have probably never heard of the *gota fría*, a phenomenon that affects these regions nearly every year.

What exactly is the *gota fría*? It is more than just heavy rain. Like hurricanes, the *gota fría* obtains its energy from the sea. Rain clouds and warm moist air build up over the sea and start to move towards the land. If this front meets a layer of cooler air over the land, it stops moving. So then the warm air rises and cools and it starts to rain. The real problem arises because the front cannot move, and more and more warm wet air accumulates. So it rains again and again and again until there is no warm moist air left.

As this phenomenon is very difficult to forecast, its consequences can be particularly devastating: rivers can burst their banks, there can be serious flooding, buildings can be badly damaged and people sometimes drown...

ANSWER THE QUESTIONS

1. Why are people from the north of Europe attracted to Spain?
2. How often does the *gota fría* occur?
3. Where does this phenomenon start?
4. Why does it rain so much?
5. Can you complete these recommendations on what to do if a *gota fría* occurs? Use as many words as you like in the answers.
   a. Stay ... and don't go out ... .
   b. You won't be able to rely on your regular source of electricity. So, make sure you have some ... in the house.
   c. If water gets into the house, switch ... and go ... .
   d. Don't go out in the car to ... .
   e. Listen to ... to find out what is happening.

Work it out

CONCEPT MAP

Use the words in the word cloud to create your own unit map in your notebook. Write any connecting texts you need.

humid subtropical, cold, gases, mesosphere, thermosphere, **layers**, oxygen, temperature, nitrogen, polar, Mediterranean, temperate, **weather**, ozone, exosphere, desert, relative humidity, **atmosphere**, alpine, troposphere, tropical, depression, zones, stratosphere, anticyclone, types, precipitation, hot, oceanic, wind, equatorial, **properties**, continental, **climate**, water vapour, atmospheric pressure

SELF-ASSESSMENT

Carry out a self-assessment of what have you learnt in this unit. Choose one answer for each question and then check your answers.

1. Most meteorological phenomena occur in the ...
   a. mesosphere
   b. troposphere
   c. stratosphere

2. What is the most abundant gas in the Earth's atmosphere?
   a. oxygen
   b. nitrogen
   c. water vapour

3. The state of the lower layers of the atmosphere at a certain time and place on Earth is called ...
   a. meteorology
   b. climate
   c. weather

4. Air always moves from ...
   a. areas of high pressure to areas of low pressure.
   b. areas of low pressure to areas of high pressure.
   c. both directions.

5. The hot climate zone is situated ...
   a. between the polar circles and the intertropical zone.
   b. between the tropics of Cancer and Capricorn.
   c. between the tropics and the polar circles.

6. Which temperate climate has mild temperatures all year round?
   a. A continental climate.
   b. A humid subtropical climate.
   c. An oceanic climate.

7. Climographs allow us to observe the annual change in ... in a specific place on the planet.
   a. temperature and precipitation.
   b. temperature and humidity.
   c. humidity and precipitation.

8. ... is found in northern Iceland, Norway and Russia.
   a. A continental climate.
   b. A polar climate.
   c. An oceanic climate.

9. What type of climate can be found throughout most of the Iberian Peninsula?
   a. A continental climate.
   b. An oceanic climate
   c. A Mediterranean climate.

10. The subtropical climate is located in the ...
    a. Islas Baleares.
    b. Islas Canarias.
    c. Islas Baleares and Islas Canarias.

06 The Earth's biomes

<< LOOKING BACK

- What is a biome?
- What types of biomes can you name?
- What types of plants can live in a desert?
- How can animals survive on the Poles?
- Are there evergreen forests on the Islas Baleares? Why or why not?
- What is an earthquake?
- What climates can you see in the biomes in the images?

Forest fires

Forest fires can have natural causes, such as lightning, volcanic eruption or spontaneous combustion. However, they can also be the result of human carelessness and accidents. Man-made fires are a threat to biodiversity and are one of the main causes of deforestation.

However, amazing as it may seem, periodic natural fires can keep a forest healthy, as they clean up the dead and decaying matter and maintain the balance of the ecosystem by removing diseased plants and harmful insects. Moreover, they help the seeds of some trees, such as pine and spruce, to germinate. After only a month, these seeds grow into little plants and 30 or 40 years after the fire, a new forest replaces the old one. In fact, experts say that forests actually need fire to regenerate – but no more often than every 50 to 100 years.

?

- What are the main causes of forest fires?
- What areas of Spain are most affected by forest fires? Why?

deciduous forest

mountain vegetation

steppe

LOOKING FORWARD

- What is a rainforest?
- What types of human activities have transformed European landscapes?
- What is the most common biome in Spain?
- What is a heat wave?
- What is a topic map and how do you interpret one?

1 The Earth's biomes

What is a rainforest?

Each area of the world that can be defined by a particular type of climate and by specific plants (flora) and animals (fauna) is called a **biome**.

1.1 Biomes in the hot zones

There are three main types of biomes in the hot zones. These biomes correspond to the three main types of hot climate.

EQUATORIAL BIOMES

Equatorial biomes are found north and south of the Equator. They include parts of Central Africa, the Amazon rainforest, some areas of Central America and the islands of Indonesia and New Guinea.

The most typical biome is the **equatorial rainforest**. In this type of rainforest there is a large number and a wide variety of plant species, especially perennials. The extraordinarily dense vegetation means that not all plants receive sunlight. Competition for sunlight causes trees to form layers at different heights. The lower layers do not have much vegetation. Plants here must adapt to conditions where there is very little light and a lot of humidity.

In the coastal areas of the equatorial region there are palm trees and mangrove swamps. These swamps contain mangrove trees, which can survive in salt water.

Rainforests have an incredible diversity of animals. There are many different species of birds, such as macaws and toucans. There are also many species of amphibians, insects, reptiles, and mammals, such as monkeys and jaguars.

Along the edges of the rainforest, vegetation is disappearing due to livestock farming and agriculture.

LAYERS OF VEGETATION IN THE RAINFOREST

Orchids, lianas and bromeliads are plants that live on the trees that reach the canopy or upper layer of vegetation. These plants have aerial roots that never touch the ground.

ACTIVITIES

1. Why do you think climate is so important in the formation of biomes?
2. In the equatorial biome, why do some plants not receive much sunlight?
3. What is the world's largest rainforest? Look at the map on the next page for help.
4. Do you think it is easy for humans to live in this biome? Give reasons for your answer.

TROPICAL BIOMES

Tropical biomes are found on both sides of the equatorial biomes, in the central plateaus of Africa, South and Central America, northern Australia and southern and southeast Asia.

The most typical biome is the **savannah**. In the wetter areas, closer to the Equator, the savannah is made up of large areas of tall grass and small woods or **isolated** trees.

In the more arid regions, the savannah has short grass, scrubland and trees, such as the baobab or the acacia, which can survive in spite of the low rainfall.

In the monsoon zones, precipitation creates the ideal conditions for monsoon forests. These are called **jungles** and contain deciduous trees, such as teak and bamboo.

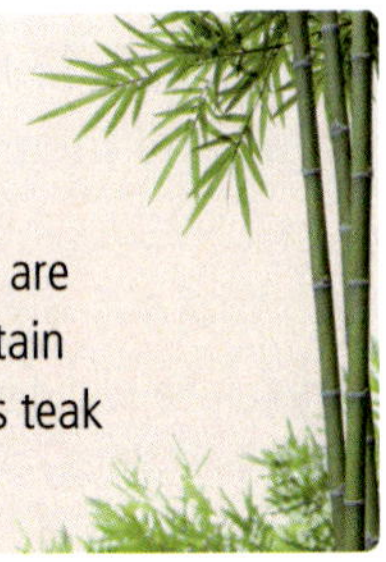

The fauna includes spectacular species: large herbivores, such as elephants and giraffes, and large carnivores, such as lions, leopards, and cheetahs.

The main economic activities are agriculture and livestock farming.

In the wet areas there are large coffee and cacao plantations.

DESERT BIOMES

Desert biomes are located near the tropics.

There are two types of desert. Temperatures in hot deserts, such as the Sahara, can reach over 50 °C. Winter temperatures in cold deserts, such as the Gobi, can fall to below 0 °C. The **scant** vegetation, such as cacti, has adapted to high temperatures and low levels of rainfall.

There is very little fauna. Only certain reptiles, insects, birds and small mammals can adapt to this **harsh** climate. However, some large animals, such as camels and dromedaries, use their **humps** to store water and fat to survive in the desert.

Human activity is only found around oases and along the edges of the desert.

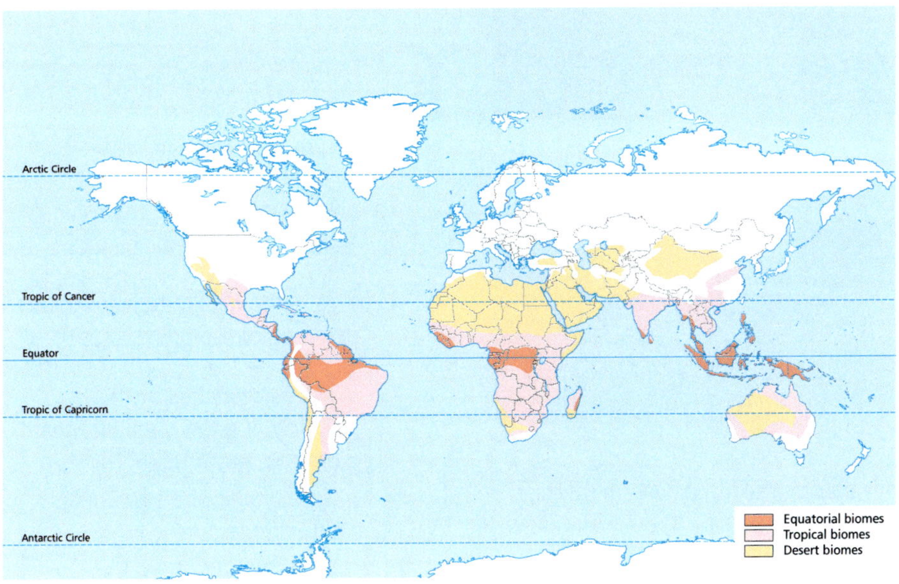

ACTIVITIES

5. How does latitude affect vegetation in the savannah? Why?
6. What is the main difference between rainforests and jungles?
7. What do all deserts have in common?
8. Look at the map and give the name of at least one desert in North America, South America, South Africa, Australia and Asia. Use an atlas to help you.

1.2 Biomes in the temperate zones

These biomes are found in regions with temperate climates. The temperatures are mild and there are four distinct seasons.

OCEANIC BIOMES

They can be found along the coasts of Western Europe, on the **shores** of the Atlantic Ocean and along some stretches of the Pacific coasts and Oceania.

The most typical biome is the **deciduous forest** biome. The most common trees are oak, beech, elm and chestnut.

In areas where the forest has been **degraded**, vegetation is made up of shrubs and scrubland. These biomes are called **moors**.

When the shrubs disappear, large areas of grass known as **oceanic grasslands** **emerge**.

The most abundant fauna are herbivores including deer, rabbits and squirrels, and predators such as bears and wolves.

Oceanic biomes have a significant human presence because of the mild climate. As a result, human activities have caused a major transformation of the natural environment.

MEDITERRANEAN BIOMES

These biomes are located in the coastal regions along the Mediterranean Sea, certain parts of the Pacific coast of the Americas, southern Africa and parts of the southern Australian coast.

The typical biome is called **Mediterranean forest**. This type of forest is made up of evergreen trees which can withstand the high temperatures of the summer months. The most common species are holm oak and cork oak.

When the Mediterranean forest deteriorates, it is sometimes replaced by areas of scrubland, with plants such as rock rose, rosemary and thyme. These types of shrubland are known as 'maquis' and 'garrigue'.

The Mediterranean biomes have been significantly transformed by humans, mostly due to farming, and more recently, tourism.

The fauna is varied. There are many herbivores such as wild boar, roe deer and hares, as well as birds such as partridge and quail. There are also predators such as foxes, lynxes and birds of prey.

ACTIVITIES

9. What are deciduous trees?
10. Why have humans greatly transformed oceanic biomes?
11. Why is the Mediterranean forest made up of evergreen trees?
12. Which activity has been transforming the Mediterranean biomes in recent times? Is this having a high or a low impact on the landscape? Give a reason for your answer.

CONTINENTAL BIOMES

These biomes cover the largest area of the Earth's surface and are typical of central Asia, Europe and North America.

The typical biome of the northern latitudes is the **taiga**. The forests are made up of evergreen trees, which can survive the low winter temperatures. The most common species are pines and firs.

To the south of the taiga, there are **continental grasslands**. When these plains of tall grass are close to desert regions, they become **steppes**, with small shrubs and short grass. The grasslands of central North America are known as plains or **prairies**.

In these biomes, there are a lot of herbivores, such as deer and wild boar. There are also **rodents**, such as squirrels and beavers, as well as predators, such as bears and wolves. Large herbivores, such as bison and horses, live on the grasslands.

One of the main human activities in continental biomes is the **timber** industry. The steppes are suitable for livestock farming and agriculture.

HUMID SUBTROPICAL BIOMES

These biomes are located in the eastern regions of Asia and America, and in Australia.

The most typical biome is the **mixed forest**. It has a lot of deciduous trees, including oak, maple and willow, along with tropical species, such as palm trees and bamboo.

The fauna is varied, with large herbivores, such as water buffalo, and large predators, such as tigers. Native species include mammals such as pandas in China and koalas in Australia.

In Argentina and Uruguay (in South America) there are extensive fertile grasslands known as 'pampas'.

Farming and industrial activities have significantly transformed these biomes.

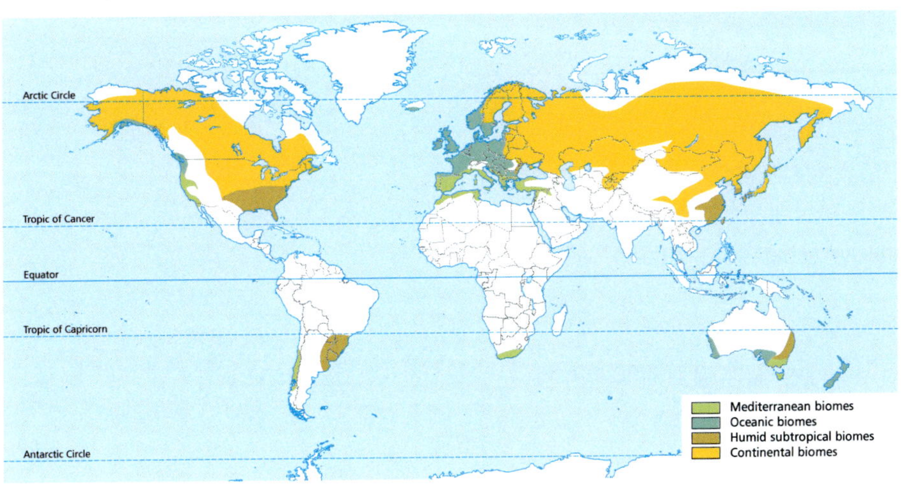

ACTIVITIES

13. Why is the taiga made up of evergreen trees?
14. When do steppes appear?
15. What is the name for grasslands in North America? And for those in South America?
16. In which climate is mixed forest found?

1.3 Biomes in the cold zones

The characteristics of the cold zones are determined by their latitude and altitude. Their latitude produces a polar climate. Their altitude creates the conditions for an alpine climate.

POLAR BIOMES

The polar biomes are located between Greenland and the northern coasts of Asia, Europe and North America in the Northern hemisphere; and in Antarctica, in the Southern hemisphere.

The landscape is white and **monotonous**, covered with permanent snow, including **vast** glaciers and ice caps. Some oceans are covered with a layer of ice called an ice field.

In the southernmost regions of the Arctic, the ice sheet melts in the summer, allowing **tundra** to form. The flora on the tundra is made up of dwarf shrubs, lichens and mosses.

Very few types of fauna can survive the icy temperatures.

In Antarctica, there are penguins and marine mammals such as elephant seals and sea lions.

The Arctic region is inhabited by seals, walruses and predators such as polar bears.

Almost all human activity is related to fishing ports in the Northern hemisphere and to scientific research in the Southern hemisphere. As a result, the biome has remained practically unchanged.

BIG THINKER

In 1994, Norwegian adventurer **Liv Arnesen** became the first woman to ski to the South Pole unaided. She skied 1 200 kilometres in 50 days. Seven years later, she and American polar explorer, Ann Bancroft, became the first women to sail and ski across Antarctica, on a 2 747 kilometre journey that took them 94 days.

POLAR ADAPTATIONS

The fauna in the Arctic region has white fur for **camouflage** in the snow. Arctic animals also have a thick layer of fat to protect them from the low temperatures.

ACTIVITIES

17. Which of the cold biomes can be found in several parts of the Earth? Why?
18. Why and where does tundra appear?
19. How do animals adapt to the polar biome? Can you think of adaptations to the environment in other biomes? List and explain them.
20. Which of the two Poles is **uninhabited**? Why is it uninhabited?

ALPINE BIOMES

Alpine biomes are found in the world's major mountain ranges. Vegetation in these biomes varies depending on the altitude. As a result, the flora is **arranged** in layers. The features of these layers depend on whether the mountain is in a temperate zone or an inter-tropical one.

Layers of vegetation in the temperate zone

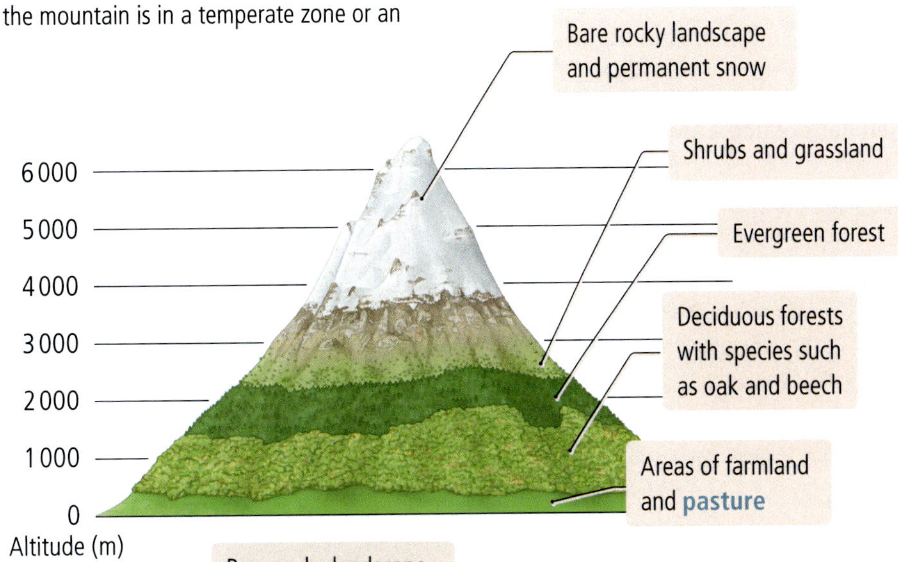

Layers of vegetation in the inter-tropical zone

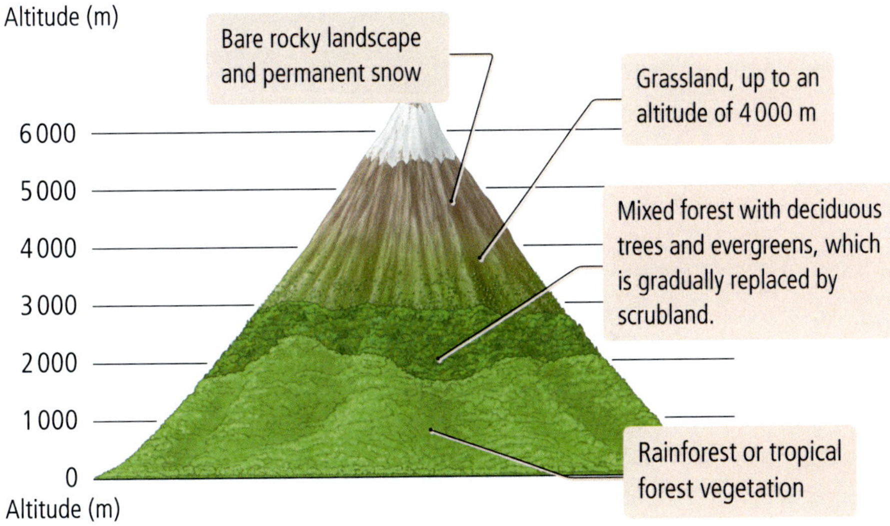

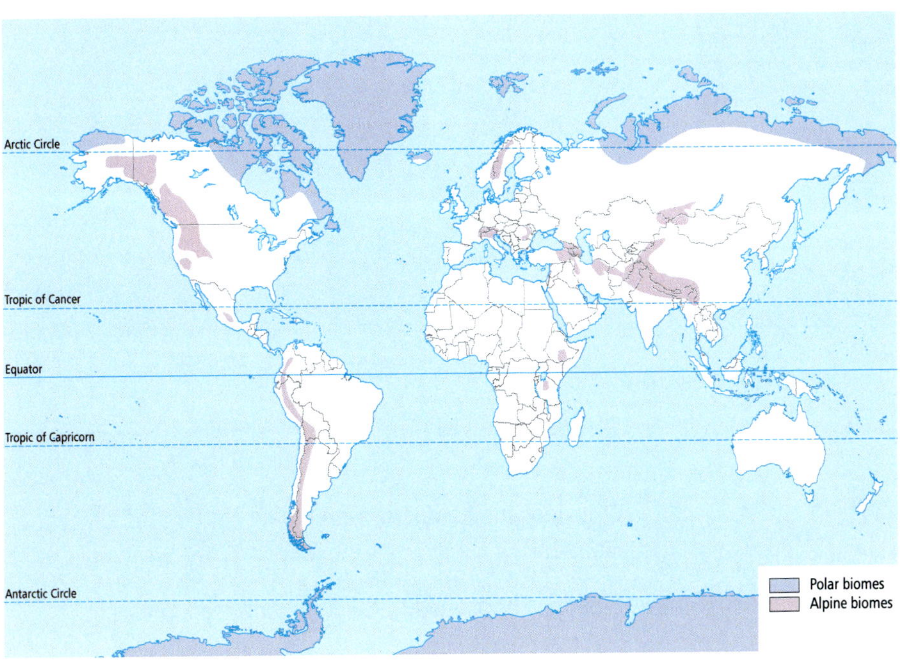

ACTIVITIES

21. Explain how and why altitude affects biomes in mountains.

22. What is the difference between the temperate zone and the inter-tropical zone as regards what appears in the upper layer? How can you explain it?

23. What kinds of plants appear at the bottom of mountains in the temperate zone?

24. Name the continents where you can find an alpine biome.

2 Biomes in Europe

Most of Europe is in the Northern hemisphere's temperate zone. However, the northernmost regions are in the Arctic Circle. These are polar environments.

All of these natural environments have been transformed by human activity, which has created different landscapes throughout Europe.

OCEANIC BIOME

This biome is found along the western coast of Europe and also **slightly** inland where there is no major geographical feature to stop the influence of rainfall from the Atlantic.

There are many deciduous forests in the coastal areas. Some regions, like the area between the mouth of the Rhine and the Seine, or southern England, are very densely populated. Almost all the original natural environment has been changed by intensive farming and industrial activities.

MEDITERRANEAN BIOME

This biome is located along the Mediterranean coast and the Atlantic coast of the Iberian Peninsula. It does not penetrate as far as central Europe because of the mountain ranges along the Mediterranean coast.

The Mediterranean forests in Europe consist of evergreen trees such as holm oak and pine. These forests have been significantly changed by humans who have transformed the land into farmland.

ACTIVITIES

25. What has been the main factor for the change in European biomes?

26. Why can we find the oceanic biome in the interior of the continent, as well as on the Atlantic coast?

27. Why does the Mediterranean biome not go through central Europe?

28. What has happened to the Mediterranean forests in Europe?

➔ What types of human activities have transformed European landscapes?

POLAR BIOME

This biome is located in northern Iceland, Norway and Russia, between the Scandinavian, Kola and Kanin Peninsulas and the Novaya Zemlya Archipelago.

The surface of the Polar region is covered in snow for most of the year. In summer, the snow disappears, allowing the tundra to form. Tundra vegetation consists of shrubs, lichens and mosses.

The harsh climate means that there is hardly any human activity, so the environment is mostly unchanged.

CONTINENTAL BIOME

This biome covers an area between the Russian Plain and the centre of the continent, where there is no maritime influence.

The plant species in the biome vary according to the latitude. The taiga is found in the Baltic regions and northern Russia. The continental grasslands are located to the south of the taiga, at a lower latitude. The steppes are found in the southernmost regions of the continent.

The natural vegetation has changed a lot due to farming activities.

ALPINE BIOME

This biome is characteristic of Europe's large mountain ranges, mainly the Caucasus Mountains, the Alps and the Pyrenees.

The vegetation varies according to the altitude. There is farmland at lower altitudes, then deciduous forests, coniferous forests, Alpine meadows and permanent snow at the highest altitudes.

Traditional livestock farming methods have not changed this biome significantly.

29. What activities do you think can be found in the alpine biome, apart from farming?

30. Using an atlas, find out the location of all the geographical features that are mentioned on this page and write their names in the map above, for example the Scandinavian peninsula, the Kola Peninsula, the Kanin Peninsula, etc.

3 Biomes in Spain

What is the most common biome in Spain?

In Spain, the biomes are influenced by the average altitude of the Peninsula and the effect of the bodies of water that surround it.

ALPINE BIOME

The location of this biome depends on the altitude and latitude of the mountain chains. There are alpine biomes starting at 1 000 m in the Cordillera Cantábrica and the Pyrenees, and above 1 500 or 2 000 m in the Sistema Ibérico, Sistema Central and Sistemas Béticos.

The vegetation grows in layers that vary according to altitude, depending on how the plants have adapted to the temperature and humidity:

1. The lowest level (800–1 200 m) has pastures and farmland.
2. The second level (1 200–1 600 m) has deciduous forest.
3. The third level (1 600–2 000 m) has coniferous forests of black pine and fir.
4. The fourth level (2 000–2 400 m) has mountain shrubs such as juniper and bilberry.
5. The fifth level (2 400–2 600 m) has alpine grassland covered with snow part of the year.
6. The upper level (above 2 600 m) is rocky with permanent snow.

The creation of a tourism infrastructure for winter sports in mountain ranges is having an increasing impact on these biomes.

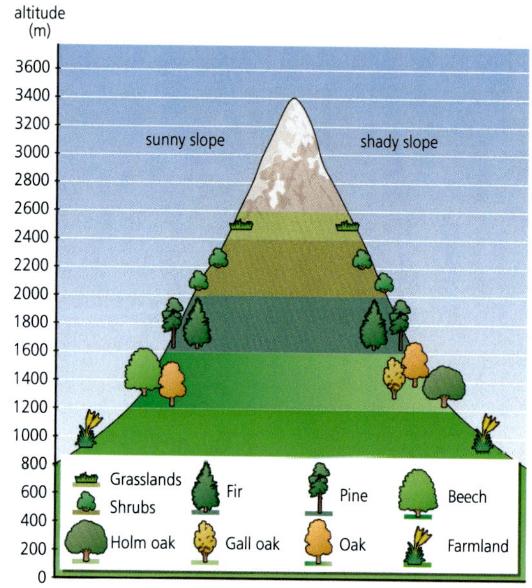

Layers of vegetation in the Pyrenees

ACTIVITIES

31. Remember the previous unit and explain the ways in which the altitude of the Peninsula and the surrounding bodies of water affect the climate.

32. Explain why alpine biomes start at a lower altitude in the Cordillera Cantábrica than in the Sistemas Béticos.

33. At which altitude can you find permanent snow in Spain? Are there any mountains taller than this altitude in your local region? Which ones?

34. Look at the diagram above. What are the differences in the vegetation between the sunny and the shady slope? What is the reason for the differences?

MEDITERRANEAN BIOMES

Most of the Iberian Peninsula and the Islas Baleares have a Mediterranean climate. However, there are differences between inland areas and the coast.

MARITIME MEDITERRANEAN BIOME

It is located on the coasts of Cataluña, Valencia, Murcia, Andalucía, the Islas Baleares, Ceuta and Melilla.

The forests are made up of evergreen trees such as holm oak, gall oak and pine, which can survive periods of **drought**. In wetter areas, there are cork oaks. In drier areas, the 'garrigue' and 'maquis' are made up of steppe species such as palmetto, esparto grass, and cactus.

CONTINENTAL MEDITERRANEAN BIOME

It is located between the Meseta and the Valle del Ebro. These regions are separated from the influence of the sea by mountain chains and the high altitude of the Meseta.

The forests are made up of evergreen trees, such as holm oak and juniper, which are resistant to cold, heat and drought. In some areas, the original forest has disappeared, giving way to shrub-like steppe vegetation such as thyme, rosemary and lavender.

In mountainous areas there are deciduous oak forests on the **shady** slopes and conifers on the sunny slopes. Along the riverbanks, there are deciduous trees such as poplar, elm and ash.

OCEANIC BIOME

The area containing this type of biome is located along the Cantabrian coast and the foot of the Pyrenees.

The vegetation is called Atlantic forest, and it is made up of deciduous trees with tall, straight trunks, such as oak, beech, chestnut and birch. In areas with poor soil or at higher altitudes, there are grasslands and moors with shrubs such as heather, gorse and blackthorn.

SUBTROPICAL BIOME

It is located on the Islas Canarias. The vegetation includes a great many regional species, such as the dragon tree, which can survive the low rainfall. At higher altitudes, there are subtropical plants such as laurisilva laurels. Above 2 000 m, there are Canary pine forests, junipers and alpine scrubland. There is no vegetation above 3 000 m.

ACTIVITIES

35. How does the amount of rainfall affect different areas in the maritime Mediterranean biome?

36. How do the Meseta and the mountain chains near coasts affect climate and landscape in the Mediterranean biome? Think back to the previous unit.

37. Name one plant native to the Islas Canarias. Why is it special?

38. Read the information about the Continental Mediterranean biome and the oceanic biome again. Where do deciduous trees appear? What climatic conditions do they need?

4 Humans and the environment

What is a heat wave?

4.1 Natural risks

Thanks to technical and scientific advances, humans have been able to adapt to the most challenging natural environments. However, when natural disasters occur, there are often terrible consequences.

INTERNAL OR TECTONIC RISKS

Earthquakes

These are violent movements of the Earth's crust that occur when tectonic plates collide. Earthquakes spread through seismic waves. An earthquake's point of origin inside the Earth is called the hypocentre. The point directly above the hypocentre, on the surface, is known as the epicentre. When earthquakes occur beneath the sea bed, they are called seaquakes. They cause tsunamis.

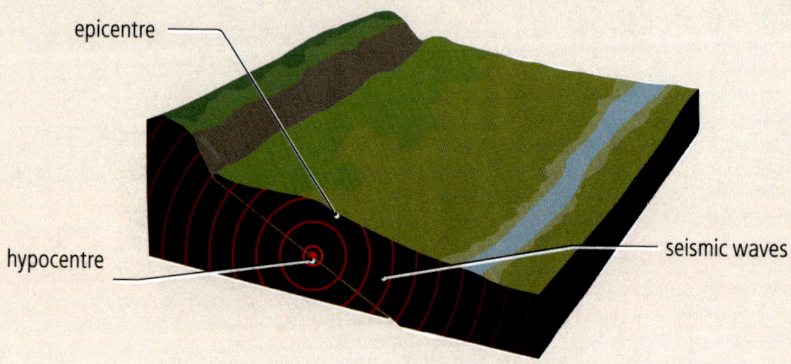

Volcanoes

These are cracks or faults on the Earth's surface through which magma emerges. Volcanic eruptions release toxic gases, solid particles, ash and lava flows that destroy crops, houses and infrastructure.

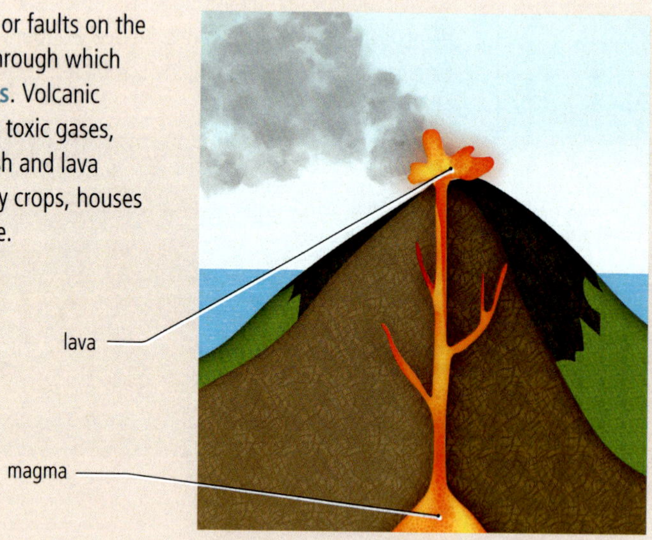

Earthquakes and volcanic eruptions can be predicted quite accurately through seismological studies. The following measures can be taken to prevent damage:

- Constructing buildings and infrastructure that can withstand tremors.
- Not building human settlements near volcanoes.
- Drawing up population protection and evacuation plans.

DID YOU KNOW?

One of the worst natural disasters in modern history was the eruption in 1883 of Krakatoa, a volcano on the Indonesian island of the same name. More than 36 000 people were killed, some by the eruption and others by the tsunamis that followed.

ACTIVITIES

39. What is the difference between the hypocentre and the epicentre?

40. Use an online newspaper library and find out when and where the three latest volcanic eruptions occurred. Then, locate them on a world map and compare it to the map of tectonic plates in Unit 2. What are the colliding plates?

41. What is a tsunami and when do they occur?

42. Think about the reasons why some people decide to live near volcanoes. Discuss them with a partner and then share your ideas with the whole class. Would you want live near one?

EXTERNAL RISKS

These risks are related to processes of erosion that alter the Earth's surface.

Landslides

Excess moisture can **weaken** a surface. If it is on a slope, landslides or rockslides can occur.

Rockfalls

Erosion breaks off fragments of rock which then fall. If the erosion affects soil, **subsidence** occurs.

These risks can be prevented through geological studies to predict possible land movements. Preventive measures include:

- Reforestation of land where plant cover has been lost.
- Construction of retaining walls.

CLIMATIC RISKS

Torrential rain

Heavy rain quickly increases the flow in rivers and causes floods. Heavy rain can also cause dams and reservoirs to break, destroying infrastructure, crops, etc.

Heat waves

These occur when temperatures are much higher than normal. Heat waves are dangerous for children, the elderly and the **infirm**. They also **exacerbate** droughts.

Cyclones, hurricanes and tornadoes

These strong winds can reach speeds of over 150 km/h.

They are powerful enough to destroy crops and buildings.

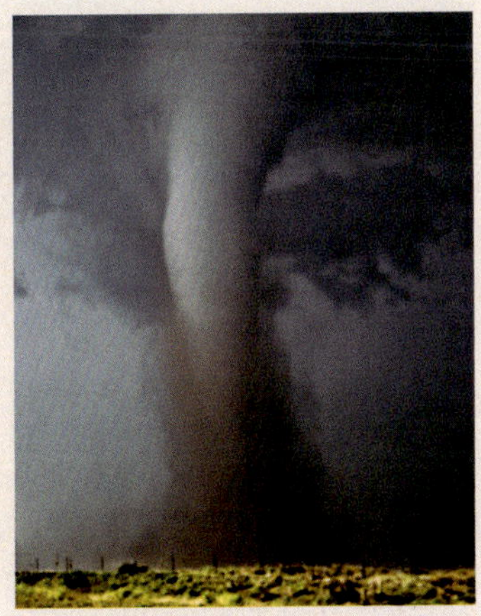

Weather risks can be predicted by analysing meteorological data. The consequences of climate disasters can be reduced through:

- Town planning regulations that prohibit the construction of houses near river beds.
- The construction of dams and drainage channels.

ACTIVITIES

43. What can be done to alleviate landslides and erosion problems?

44. What are the consequences of heat waves? Distinguish between human and physical consequences.

45. Do some research and find out the difference between cyclones, hurricanes and tornadoes. Also look up the meaning of the word typhoon: when do we use this word?

46. Now that you know more about cyclones, are they likely to happen in Spain? Give a reason for your answer.

47. Describe one way of reducing erosion risks and another one of reducing climatic risks.

4.2 Environmental risks

Throughout history, the Earth's climate has changed naturally on several occasions. However, the current rate of global warming appears to be largely caused by pollution and the overexploitation of natural resources. Human demographic and economic development in recent centuries has also altered the natural condition of the Earth. These processes are the cause of various types of natural risk.

AIR POLLUTION

Acid rain

Some industrial activities result in the release of toxic gases into the atmosphere. These gases combine with water vapour in the air to form dangerous acids such as sulphuric or nitric acids. These substances fall to the Earth's surface in the form of acid rain, destroying vegetation, eroding stone buildings and monuments, and polluting the water and soil.

Destruction of the ozone layer

Ozone is a gas that forms a layer in the stratosphere that absorbs the ultraviolet radiation from sunlight. In recent decades, the use of certain aerosols has released gases such as CFCs into the atmosphere. These gases destroy the ozone layer. The increase in ultraviolet radiation is a serious health risk for all living creatures.

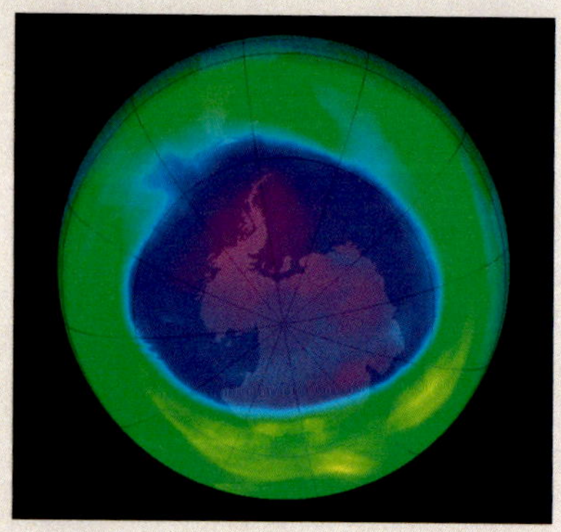

Greenhouse effect

Industrial activity, vehicles and forest fires release large amounts of pollutant gases into the atmosphere. These gases prevent heat from escaping from the Earth's surface, causing an increase in temperature. This process is called the greenhouse effect. It contributes to climate change.

Smog

Industrial activities and traffic in large cities cause pollutants and particles to accumulate in the air. During a long period of high pressure (anticyclone), a cloud of pollution forms. This is called smog. Smog causes serious breathing problems and contributes to the greenhouse effect.

ACTIVITIES

48. Is there a natural greenhouse effect? If so, is it good for human life? Explain your answers.

49. What are some of the health consequences of the ozone layer depletion for humans?

50. What human activity is responsible for acid rain?

51. What is smog and what is it due to? When and where does it appear?

WATER POLLUTION

Industry, farming and urban activities generate large amounts of toxic waste and waste water. When this pollution reaches rivers, lakes and seas, it kills some animal species, causes harmful algae to develop and makes large amounts of surface and underground water undrinkable.

Oil tanker accidents cause oil spills. Marine animals get trapped in the oil, which also pollutes fishing resources and endangers coastal ecosystems and populations.

SOIL POLLUTION

Urban and domestic waste that is not recycled or processed is disposed of in uncontrolled **landfills**. This rubbish includes products such as bleach, detergents, plastics and batteries. These pollute the soil and underground aquifers.

The indiscriminate use of chemical fertilisers and insecticides in the agricultural sector causes soil pollution and affects ecosystems.

OVEREXPLOITATION OF NATURAL RESOURCES

Overexploitation through crop and livestock farming exhausts soil nutrients and prevents plant growth. Excessive logging and forest fires also destroy plant cover. All of these activities can cause soil erosion and desertification.

Overexploitation through crop and livestock farming and logging destroys natural forests and has caused many plant and animal species to disappear or be in danger of extinction.

Indiscriminate hunting and the trade of exotic species are also a problem.

ACTIVITIES

52. What are some of the everyday products that sometimes pollute the soil and aquifers?

53. Do some research. Have there been any oil spills in Spain that have affected its coasts? If so, when and where?

54. What is meant by an indiscriminate use of chemicals and pesticides? Why do you think farmers use these substances this way?

55. Explain the difference between deforestation and desertification. What are the common causes of both processes?

Discovery techniques

Creating and reading topic maps

Topic maps show specific information about a particular geographical area. In other words, topic maps combine two types of information: cartographical information (to identify the area analysed) and information about the phenomenon studied. This information can be qualitative (e.g. crop type) or quantitative (e.g. population density).

How do you make a topic map?

To make a topic map showing the vegetation in Spain's different natural environments, follow the steps below.

1. Decide what type of map you want to use. The most frequent maps are:

   - **Isoline maps.** These delimit areas using lines connecting several points with the same value. For example, maps showing atmospheric pressure use isobars that connect points with the same pressure.

     On some isoline maps, such as weather maps or plant landscape maps, the spaces between the lines are different colours.

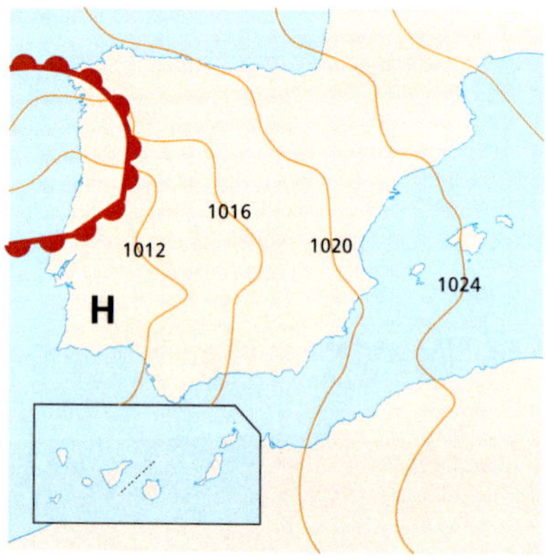

Isobar map showing atmospheric pressure

   - **Choropleth maps.** These use lines marking pre-established administrative, political or physical boundaries. These maps show quantitative or proportional values of a single economic, demographic, urban or political phenomenon. Different values or intensities are marked using different colours or patterns.

     These maps also use other elements, such as icons, to provide information.

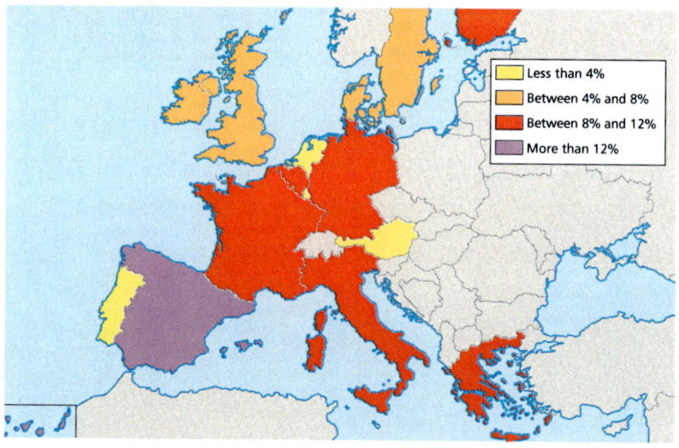

Choropleth map showing unemployment in the EU in 2002

2. Now follow these steps:

   a. Draw an outline map of the area studied.

   b. Collect the geographical information you want to show. You can find this information in the sections on biomes in Spain and on the map on page 112.

   - Climate: Continental Mediterranean, Maritime Mediterranean, Oceanic, Alpine and Subtropical.
   - The most important plant species for each natural environment:

Continental Mediterranean	Holm oak, poplar, elm, ash, pine, oak, holly, heather, strawberry tree, thyme, rosemary, lavender...
Maritime Mediterranean	Coastal holm oak, Portuguese oak, pine, cork oak, palmetto, esparto grass, thyme, cactus, prickly pear...
Atlantic	Oak, beech, chestnut, birch, heather, gorse, blackthorn...
Alpine	Black pine, fir, juniper, bilberry...
Subtropical	Canary Island spurge, dragon tree, heather, laurisilva laurel, Canary pine, Canary juniper, broom...

This information can be simplified. For example, you can categorise Mediterranean shrubs as steppe vegetation, and Atlantic shrubs as moor vegetation. Shrubs in high mountain and subtropical climates can be categorised as high-mountain shrubs.

3. Now draw the map.

- Vegetation maps use isolines. On the outline map, draw isolines to delimit the different biomes in Spain. Use the map on page 112 to help you. Now fill in each area with a different colour. The different colours will be shown in the key.
- Create an icon for each plant species. These icons will be included in the key and drawn on the map based on the information you have gathered.

Do not rely solely on the data collected, but also on the source of that data. For example, this might remind you that typical trees in continental Mediterranean environments grow on river banks, so they are not found in areas where steppe shrubs grow.

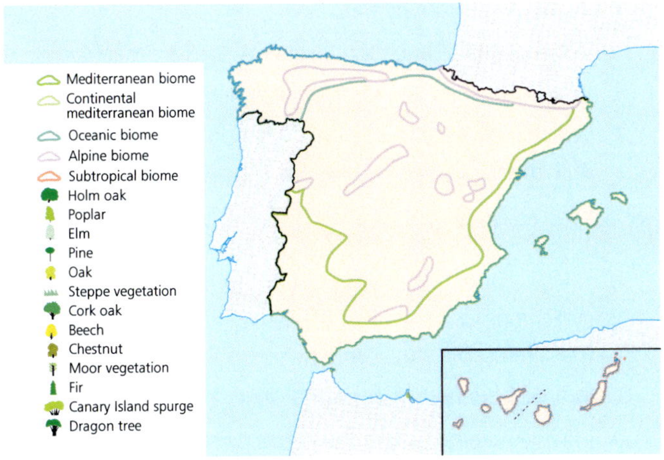

Reading and interpretation

By interpreting topic maps, you can study the phenomenon represented. Follow these steps:

- Define the phenomenon represented.
- Delimit the geographical area and the spatial distribution of that phenomenon.
- Explain the values shown and relate them to the context.

In this case, you would need to explain that the map shows the vegetation in all of Spain's natural environments. The plant species vary widely in different parts of the Iberian Peninsula and its archipelagos because they are influenced by altitude, latitude and a range of climates. As there are many different climates in Spain, the country's vegetation is varied.

However, human activities have destroyed many areas of natural vegetation over the course of several centuries.

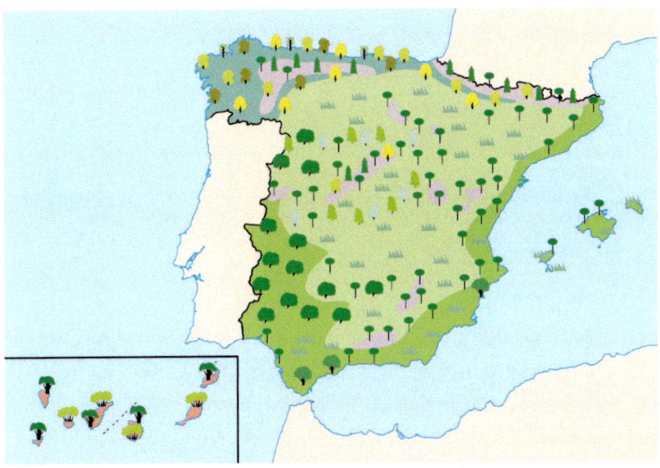

Practise what you've learnt

Create and interpret a vegetation map of Europe based on the maps on pages 108 and 109, and on the following data:

Natural environment	Plant species
Oceanic or Atlantic	Oak, beech, chestnut, moor shrubs
Continental	Pine, fir, continental steppe vegetation
Mediterranean	Holm oak, cork oak, pine, steppe shrubs
Alpine	Fir, black pine, high-mountain shrubs
Polar	Tundra vegetation

Revision activities

1 Answer the questions.

a. What is a biome?
b. How can you explain the abundance of living beings in the rainforest?
c. At which latitude do deserts appear more frequently?
d. What are deciduous trees?
e. Which kinds of animals can survive in the desert?
f. Why do alpine biomes differ according to the latitude?
g. Which biome is the most densely populated in Europe, and why?

2 Identify the biome:

a. Which biome is characterised by dryness?
b. Which one is made up of a few types of evergreen trees that are used for the timber industry?
c. In which biomes do deciduous trees appear?
d. In which biome would you find a monsoon forest?
e. In which biome are there more animals with white fur?
f. Which biome has plants that only grow a few centimetres?
g. Which biome receives the most rainfall?
h. Which biome is characterised by the presence of mangrove trees?
i. Which biome only appears in the Northern hemisphere?
j. Which biome appears between deserts and grasslands?

3 Biomes: extension activities.

a. Group work. In groups, choose one of the biomes. You are going to do some research and then, present your biome to the class with a poster. On this poster, remember to include information on the following: name of biome, animals and plants, location, human activity and main characteristics. Use photos, pictures and maps!
b. Choose one animal from one of the biomes that you didn't study. Could this animal live in the one your group presented? Why or why not?

4 Look at these photos and identify the environmental issue that has caused each of them. Next, explain what human activities are at the root of these problems.

5 Read the following text about the earthquake that took place in Nepal in 2015 and then answer the questions:

"Why was the earthquake in Nepal such a devastating event?

Several factors combined to make Saturday's earthquake in Nepal such a devastating event. The first was its basic magnitude. At 7.8 on the Richter scale, this was one of the most powerful earthquakes to strike the region in the past 80 years. In addition, it was a shallow event with a source that was only 11km below ground.

That has special consequences, according to David Rothery, professor of planetary geosciences at the Open University. "The shallowness of the source made the ground-shaking at the surface worse than it would have been for a deeper earthquake," he explained. "I've seen pictures of poorly constructed old buildings destroyed in Kathmandu, and I'm concerned that in this mountainous region there could have been landslides that might have destroyed or cut off various remote villages." As to the specific cause of the earthquake, it was triggered by the India tectonic plate, which is moving northwards at the rate of 5cm a year into central Asia."

Robin McKie, The Guardian, Sunday 26 April 2015

Questions:

a. What caused the earthquake?
b. How does the Richter scale show that this earthquake was devastating?
c. How did the location of the hypocentre affect the size of the earthquake?
d. How does Professor Rothery describe the houses in the Nepali capital? How can this affect the impact of the earthquake?
e. Re-read the information about the measures that can be taken to prevent damages from this kind of natural disaster. Bearing in mind that Nepal is one of the poorest countries in the world, do you think it is possible to implement them there? Give reasons for your answer.
f. After reading the passage, do you think other earthquakes will occur in this area? Give a reason for your answer.

6 An earthquake has many destructive effects. Can you distinguish between primary effects, that happen immediately because of the earth's movements, and secondary ones, that are a consequence of the damage? Write a P, for a primary effect or an S, for a secondary one, next to each of these effects:

a. Many people were left homeless.
b. Many buildings were destroyed.
c. Some bridges and roads collapsed.
d. Electricity supplies, as well as gas and water, were disrupted.
e. Some industries were forced to close.
f. Several trains were derailed.

7 Look at these photos and identify the biomes. Then, say where in the world each photo could have been taken.

8 Read the following text and do the activities.

"Living near a volcano is very dangerous, but there are some advantages to living close to an area of volcanic activity. For instance, the soil there is very good for agriculture and contains many raw materials, like minerals. Recently, tourism has provided a lot of money because tourists want to see geysers or enjoy hot springs in those areas. People also live near volcanoes when they have always lived there or don't have enough money to move elsewhere. And many believe scientists will predict eruptions in time to avoid the dangers."

Activities:

a. Make a T-chart and list the advantages of living near a volcano in one column, and the disadvantages in the other column.
b. Are there more advantages or disadvantages?
c. In your opinion, do the advantages outweigh the disadvantages, or is it the other way round?

9 Find out the environmental consequences regarding climate change and what is being done about it.

a. Using the Global Awareness Layer in Google Earth (https://www.google.com/earth/), tick the box UNEP: Atlas of Our Changing Environment.
b. Explore the map and look for places that have been altered as a consequence of climate change.
c. Choose three of those places in different continents and read the information the UNEP (United Nations Environment Programme) provides about them. Answer these questions:

   i. Where are they? (Be specific)

   ii. What changes can be observed in the photos?

   iii. What problems could these changes cause the environment?

   iv. What are the causes of these changes?

d. Present the information to your class. If possible, find some more photographs and show them to your class.

Read and think

CLIMATE CHANGE AND LIFE ON EARTH

Climate change is more than changes in the weather. Climate affects the environment that living things depend on. Non-living things essential to living things, such as soil, rocks, oceans, and lakes, are also affected by climate change.

Any change in the climate of an area can affect the plants and animals living there, as well as the whole ecosystem. Some species are already responding to warmer temperatures by moving to cooler locations. Climate change also alters the life cycles of plants and animals. As temperatures get warmer, many plants are growing and blooming earlier, and living longer. Some animals are coming out of hibernation sooner or migrating at different times from usual.

Global warming is affecting the whole world but, at the moment, its most serious impacts are in polar and alpine regions. Polar bears in the Arctic spend most of their time on sea ice, which is their main habitat. The ice provides a platform for them for hunting, living and breeding. But, now, warmer temperatures are affecting the amount of sea ice and its thickness and age. If there is less ice, the remaining ice melts more quickly.

Moreover, sea ice forms an entire ecosystem inhabited by plankton and micro-organisms, which support a rich food chain that feeds seals, which are prey for polar bears. Many species in the polar bear's food chain are adapted to life on or under the ice: the algae that grows on the bottom of 'old' ice, as well as invertebrates, birds, fish and seals. If the polar bear's habitat disappears, most of the living things in its ecosystem will too. And polar bears will have to move and also change their diets…

ANSWER THE QUESTIONS

1. Why is climate change more than just changes in the weather?
2. What non-living things do living things depend on?
3. How are some plants and animals responding to climate change?
4. Which biomes are currently most affected by global warming?
5. How are warmer temperatures affecting sea ice?
6. Work in pairs or small groups. Choose a biome and find out about one of the following.
   a. Living and non-living things in danger.
   b. Preserving or creating a habitat.

   Present your findings to the class.

Work it out

CONCEPT MAP

Use the words in the word cloud to create your own unit map in your notebook. Write any connecting texts you need.

risks mangrove swamp rockfalls natural alpine hot zones
equatorial climatic rainforest mediterranean forest
savannah tectonic
water pollution moor taiga
Biomes landslides
grassland continental
jungle torrential rain
air pollution humid subtropical
Mediterranean environmental forest
desert
soil pollution tundra polar cold zones mixed forest external earthquakes
oceanic heat waves tropical temperate zones volcanoes
evergreen forest overexploitation of natural resources hurricanes

SELF-ASSESSMENT

Carry out a self-assessment of what you have learnt in this unit. Choose one answer for each question and then check your answers.

1. A biome is defined by a particular type of ...
   a. climate, flora and fauna.
   b. weather, fauna and vegetation.
   c. climate and human activity.

2. The savannah is the most typical ...
   a. desert biome.
   b. equatorial biome.
   c. tropical biome.

3. Where can we find large predators such as tigers?
   a. In oceanic biomes.
   b. In continental biomes.
   c. In humid subtropical biomes.

4. The Mediterranean forest is made up of trees such as ...
   a. oak, beech, elm and chestnut.
   b. holm and cork oak.
   c. pine, fir and bamboo.

5. The cold zones are determined by their ...
   a. climate.
   b. flora and fauna.
   c. latitude and altitude.

6. Vegetation in alpine biomes varies depending on the ...
   a. climate.
   b. altitude.
   c. the level of human activity.

7. What type of biome is found along the western coast of Europe?
   a. Continental biome.
   b. Mediterranean biome.
   c. Oceanic biome.

8. The steppes are found in ...
   a. the southernmost regions of Europe.
   b. the northernmost regions of Europe.
   c. the Alps and the Pyrenees.

9. The most typical biome of the Iberian Peninsula is the ...
   a. continental biome.
   b. Mediterranean biome.
   c. oceanic biome.

10. The current rate of global warming appears to be largely caused by ...
    a. pollution.
    b. volcanoes.
    c. heat waves.

Glossary

A

Aborigine (n): a member of the race of people with dark skins who were the first people to live in Australia

Accurately (adv): without error, precise, and meticulous

Aim (n): the purpose of doing something

Alluvial (adj): earth and sand that has been left by rivers, floods

Alluvial plain (n): a level or gently sloping flat or a slightly undulating land surface resulting from the repeated deposition of alluvial materials by running water

Arid (adj): very dry and without enough rain

Arranged (v): organised

Astronomer (n): a scientist who studies stars, planets, comets, galaxies and celestial objects

Average (n): a standard or level that is considered to be typical or usual

Axis (n): GEOMETRY an imaginary, central line around which an object turns

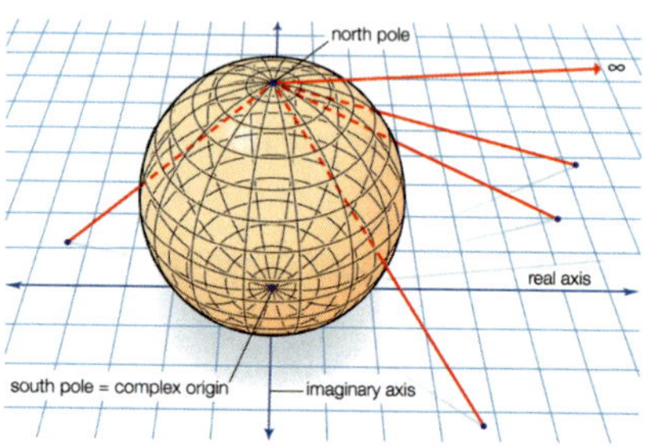

Axis

B

Basin (n): a circular or oval valley or natural depression on the Earth's surface, especially one containing water

Bathymetry (n): the study of the floors of waterbodies, including the ocean, rivers and lakes

Blissfully (adv): in a way that makes you happy or that prevents unpleasant things from affecting you

Boundaries (n): real or imagined lines that mark the limits or edges of something and separate it from other things or places

C

Challenging (adj): difficult in a way that tests your ability or determination

Chiefly (adv): in general; mainly; mostly

Clay (n): thick, heavy soil that is soft when wet, and hard when dry or baked, used for making bricks and containers

Coastline (n): the particular shape of the coast, seen from the sea or on a map

Collide (v): to hit something violently

Coordinate (n): one of a pair of numbers or letters that show the exact position of a point on a map or graph

Course (n): the path or channel along which the water of a river or stream moves

Coves (n): small bays; areas of sea that are partly surrounded by land

Coves

Crevices(n): small, narrow cracks or spaces, especially in the surface of a rock or wall

D

Dashed (adj): having gaps or spaces

Deal (n): an agreement or an arrangement

Debris (n): a collection of loose material derived from rocks

Degrade (v): be reduced by erosion or down-cutting

Den (n): the hidden home of some types of wild animal

Dictate (v): to give orders, or tell someone exactly what they must do, with total authority

Distinct (adj): clearly separate and different from something else

Distorted (adj): changed from the usual, original, natural, or intended form

Downhill (adv): (moving) towards the bottom of a hill

Drought (n): a long period of time when there is little or no rain

E

Eel (n): a long, thin, snake-like fish

Elliptical (adj): oval shape

Elongated (adj): long and thin, often in a way that is not usual

Emerge (v): start; to exist; to appear

Equidistant (adj): equally far or close

Equinox (n): either of the two occasions in the year when day and night are of equal length

Erod (v): to slowly reduce or destroy something

Erosive (adj): tending to erode or cause erosion (erosion is the act or process of wearing away by water, wind, or other natural agents)

Erosion

Evenly (adv): equal in number, measure or amount.

Exacerbate (v): to make something that is already bad even worse

Exceed (v): to go past an allowed limit

Exert (v): to apply a force

F

'49ers (n): gold seekers who travelled to California in 1849

Feature (n): an important part of something or a quality

Fierce (adj): strong and powerful

Fissure (n): a deep, narrow crack in rock or the earth

Flat (adj): smooth, with no curved

Flooding (n): a situation in which an area is covered with water, especially from rain

Flooding

Flow (n): the steady and continuous movement of a river or a stream in one direction

Fold (v): to bend

Furthest (adv): far

G

Gender (n): the physical and/or social condition of being male or female

Geographer (n): a person who studies geography

Geoid (n): a model of the Earth's shape based on a hypothetical surface that closely approximates global mean sea level.

Geophysicist (n): someone who studies the Earth using gravity, magnetic, electrical, and seismic methods.

Geysers (n): pools of hot water that send columns of water and steam into the air on a regular or irregular basis

Geysers

Grid (n): a structure made from horizontal and vertical lines crossing each other to form squares

H

Harsh (adj): very difficult and unpleasant to live in

Havoc (n): a situation in which there is a lot of damage, destruction or confusion

Heavily (adv): in large amounts

Hectopascal (n): a metric measurement unit of pressure (one hectopascal (hPa) is equivalent to one millibar and the unit is commonly used to measure atmospheric pressure)

Hospitable (adj): having a climate or environment that allows things to grow and/or live

I

Infirm (n): ill or weak often because of old age

Inhabitants (n): a person or animal that lives in a particular place

Inlet (n): a narrow channel or strip of water that goes from a sea or lake into the land, or between islands

Inner (adj): inside

Intervals (n): spaces between two points

Isolated (adj): alone, far away from other things

Itinerary (n): a plan of a journey, including the route and the places to be visited

L

Lagoon (n): a lake of salt water that is separated from the sea by a coral reef or an area of rock or sand

Landfills (n): places where large amounts of waste material are buried under the earth

Landfills

Lawlessly (adv): not controlled by laws, or illegal

Layer (n): a sheet, quantity, or thickness of material, typically one of several, covering a surface or body.

Low-lying (adj): at low elevation; lower than its surroundings

M

Made up (adj): invented

Marsh (n): ground near a lake, a river, or the sea that often floods and is always wet

Meanders (n): winding curves or bends of a river

Melted (adj): having turned soft or into a liquid

Mild (adj): mild weather is not very cold or not as cold as usual

Glossary

Molten (adj): in a liquid state because of being heated to a very high temperature

Monotonous (adj): not changing and therefore boring

Mountaineering (n): the sport or activity of climbing mountains

N

Narrow (adj): having a small distance from one side to the other, especially in comparison with the length

Narrow

Navigable (adj): wide, deep or safe enough for ships and boats to sail on

O

Orbit (n): the curved path followed by a planet, satellite, comet, etc. as it moves around another celestial body under the influence of gravitation

Outer (adj): at a greater distance from the centre

P

Pasture (n): area of land covered in grass or similar plants suitable for feeding animals such as cows and sheep

Peak (adj): characterised by maximum activity

Peak (n): the pointed top of a mountain, or the mountain itself

Phenomena (n): facts or events in nature, especially unusual or interesting things that can be observed

Pictorially (adv): shown in the form of a picture or photograph

Picturesque (adj): pretty, especially in a way that looks old-fashioned

Piles (n): masses of something that have been placed somewhere

Plot (v): to mark out a number of points on a graph

Porous (adj): having many small holes that allow water or air to pass through slowly

Predominate (v): to prevail, to be the most important

Projection (n): the representation of a line, figure, or solid on a given plane as it would be seen from a particular direction

Protractor (n): an instrument for measuring and drawing angles, usually made from a half circle of transparent plastic with degrees (0° to 180°) marked on it

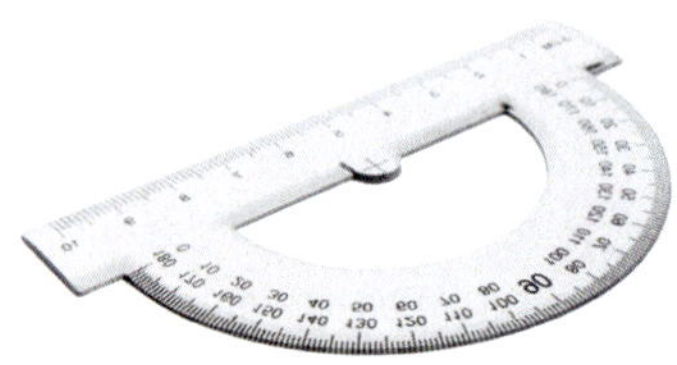

Protractor

R

Rainfall (n): rain, or the amount of rain that falls

Ratio (n): the relationship between two numbers that shows the number of times one of them contains (or is contained within the other)

Revolve (v): to move around a central point or axis

Ridge (n): a long, narrow raised part of a surface, especially a high edge along a mountain or a line of hills

Rodent (n): any of various small mammals with large, sharp front teeth, such as mice, rats, hamsters, etc.

Rodent

Rotate (v): to move, turn or cause something to turn in a circle, especially around a fixed point

S

Sandbank (n): a raised area of sand below the surface of the sea or a river that can only be seen when the water level is low

Scant (adj): insufficient, very little and not enough

Shallower (adj): comparative of the adjective shallow. Having little depth

Sheets (n): wide surfaces

Slopes (n): areas of land with a natural incline that are part of a mountain or hill

Solstice (n): an astronomical event that occurs twice each year (in June and December) as the Sun reaches its highest or lowest excursion relative to the celestial equator on the celestial sphere.

Solstice at Stonehenge

Spatial (adj): relating to space

Split into (v): to divide

Stable (adj): firmly fixed or not likely to move or change

Steeper (adj): comparative of the adjective 'steep' meaning having a slope or gradient approaching the perpendicular

Straight (adj, adv): continuing in one direction without bending or curving

Strictly (adv): exactly or correctly

Subsidence (n): the process by which land sinks to a lower level

Sunken (adj): at a lower level than the surrounding area

Swamp (n): an area of ground flooded with water in which plants are growing

T

Terrain (n): an area of land, especially with regard to its physical features

Timber (n): wood that is prepared for use in construction

Timber

Tiny (adj): extremely small

Torrential (adj): used to refer to very heavy rain

Trade winds (n): constant easterly winds that dominate most of the tropics and subtropics throughout the world, blowing mainly from the northeast in the Northern hemisphere, and from the southeast in the Southern hemisphere

Tremor (n): a small earthquake during which the ground shakes slightly

Trench (n): a long deep narrow hole in the ocean floor

Tributary (n): a river or stream that flows into a larger river or a lake

Troughs (n): small valleys

Trough

U

Undulate (v): to have a continuous up and down shape or movement, like waves on the sea

Undulating (adj): describing or having small hills and slopes that look like waves

Uninhabited (adj): with no people living there

Unspoiled (adj): not spoiled, in particular (of a place), changed or damaged by people

Unstable (adj): not solid and firm and therefore not strong, safe, or likely to last

V

Vast (adj): of very great extent or quantity; immense

Viscous (adj): having a thick, sticky consistency between solid and liquid

W

Warm up (v): if an event warms up, it starts to become more interesting, enjoyable, or exciting

Waterfall (n): water, especially from a river or stream, dropping from a higher to a lower point, sometimes from a great height

Watersheds (n): areas of high ground from which water flows down to a river

Watershed

Well (n): a deep hole in the ground from which you can get water, oil, or gas

Well

Name: Heidi Hammel

Lived: 1960–present day

Nationality: American

Interests: Planetary science, astronomy, geology

Bright ideas: Hammel is a planetary astronomer with a special interest in Neptune and Uranus. Thanks to her research, she has promoted the general public's understanding of planetary science. She has been awarded with prizes from different scientific associations and, in 2003, she was recognised as one of the 50 most important women in science.

Name: James Cook

Lived: 1728–1779

Nationality: British

Interests: Cartography

Bright ideas: Cook was an explorer and navigator, and also captain in the Royal Navy. He made maps of Newfoundland before travelling to the Pacific Ocean when he made the first recorded circumnavigation of New Zealand. He left a legacy of geographical knowledge, very useful for his successors exploring the same field.

Name: Emilio Herrera

Lived: 1879–1967

Nationality: Spanish

Interests: Physics, aeronautics

Bright ideas: Herrera was a military engineer, physicist and politician. After graduating from a military academy, he researched aeronautics. In 1936, Herrera designed a pressurised uniform for air balloon and airship explorations. Later on, the NASA used his design to develop modern space suits. He was president in exile of the government of the Spanish Republic.

Name: Alfred Wegener

Lived: 1880–1930

Nationality: German

Interests: Meteorology, geology, astronomy

Bright ideas: Although during his lifetime he was primarily known for his achievements in meteorology and as a pioneer of polar investigation, nowadays he is most widely recognised for his theory of continental drift. In 1912, he hypothesised that continents slowly drift around the Earth, but the idea was not accepted until the 1950s when other discoveries such as palaeomagnetism provided strong support for his theory.

Name: Ramón Margalef

Lived: 1919–2004

Nationality: Spanish

Interests: Biology, ecology

Bright ideas: Margalef was the first professor of ecology in Spain. Many of his publications consolidated him as one of the fathers of modern ecology. In recognition of his contribution to ecological research, he received numerous scientific international awards and some Spanish ones such as the Ramón y Cajal Award, and the Gold Medal of the Generalitat of Catalunya.

Name: Liv Arnesen

Lived: 1953–present day

Nationality: Norwegian

Interests: Education, skiing

Bright ideas: Arnesen is an educator and adventurer. She is known for being the first female to ski unaided to the South Pole, which she did in 1994. Arnesen is also a motivational speaker and collaborates with corporations and non-profit organisations around the world. She has received many awards and diplomas of honour from different geographic societies and associations.